Becoming Your Husband's Best Friend

Lisa & David Frisbie

HARVEST HOUSE PUBLISHERS

EUGENE, OREGON

Scripture quotations are from the Good News Translation—Second Edition © 1992 by American Bible Society. Used by permission.

Cover by Koechel Peterson & Associates, Inc.

Cover photo © 2010 Steve Sant and World of Stock

This book contains stories in which the author has changed people's names and some details of their situations in order to protect their privacy.

BECOMING YOUR HUSBAND'S BEST FRIEND
Copyright © 2010 by Lisa and David Frisbie
Published by Harvest House Publishers
Eugene, Oregon 97402
www.harvesthousepublishers.com

Library of Congress Cataloging-in-Publication Data
  Frisbie, Lisa
  Becoming your husband's best friend / Lisa and David Frisbie.
     p. cm.
  ISBN 978-0-7369-2921-9 (pbk.)
  1. Wives—Religious life. 2. Marriage—Religious aspects—Christianity. I. Frisbie, David II. Title.
  BV4528.15.F75 2010
  248.8'44—dc22
                                                                    2010021738

Printed in the United States of America

          10 11 12 13 14 15 16 17 18 / LB-SK / 10 9 8 7 6 5 4 3 2 1

Dedication

This book is dedicated to four of the many couples who have shown us what grace, intimacy, togetherness, and partnership are all about. They have lived marriage well.

Our pastor, Dr. Paul Cunningham, taught us about marriage as we began our life together. Our lives are permanently altered because our journey intersected with his. His wife, Dr. Connie Cunningham, taught our early-married Sunday school class. Much of the wisdom in the pages of our books can be traced to Connie's witty, insightful teaching.

Our close friends Arthur and Mattie Uphaus were tremendous examples for us. Mattie modeled for us the gracious spirit and loving heart of a transformational wife. In almost three decades of knowing Mattie we never heard her utter one negative word, make one critical comment (even in jest), or say any unpleasant thing about her husband. Mattie showed us the power of positive living. Both she and Arthur are now in heaven.

Much of what we know about healthy and godly marriage, both of us learned at home. We each knew that our parents loved God, loved each other, and loved us. Divorce was commonplace among our peers, but we knew that it was not even remotely a possibility for our parents. Through difficulty and stress, in good times and bad, our parents demonstrated the meaning of commitment.

Lee and Marilyn Frisbie, married 58 years at this writing, have taught us many lessons about life and ministry. They have modeled a loving, caring, God-honoring marriage relationship in genuine and helpful ways. They have supported their pastors, led youth ministry across several generations, and ministered to missionaries, seminary students, and others, sharing from lives of faithful integrity.

Lamont and Ruth Jacobson, Lisa's parents, have shown us what a committed Christian couple looks like up close. They are young at heart and fully engaged in living. We recently helped them celebrate their sixtieth anniversary, which was held in a church they still serve. Ruth is the worship leader in her church, active as ever. Mom and Dad Jacobson love God, love each other, and love us. We admire their energy and enthusiasm!

These are four of the many couples whose inspiring marriages challenged us to follow their wise examples. Although they could and did guide us with their words and their teaching, we learned the most by watching them "do life" together. To this day we reflect on, learn from, and strive to follow the powerful examples of these four couples. As we celebrate 32 years together, we owe a great debt of gratitude to each of them.

As we work to make marriages healthier and stronger, to help couples succeed and thrive, and to help families stay together and be healthy, we are "paying it forward" because we have received so much from others.

To Paul, Connie, Arthur, Mattie, Lee, Marilyn, Lamont, and Ruth, thank you for walking the walk while you were talking the talk. We're a little bit behind you on this journey of life, but we're following in your footsteps with joy and gladness.

Acknowledgments

We wrote this book as we traveled the world, carrying out our God-given ministry of speaking, teaching, training, and counseling. Because of the complexity of our travel schedule, several of these chapters were written in locations as culturally diverse as Balchik and Broken Arrow, as geographically separated as Oahu and Orlando. Portions of this book were written on three different continents and in many different cities, towns, and villages.

From beginning to end, we were aided by family and friends, hosts and guides, an eclectic mix of spiritually minded persons who served as midwives in the birth of this book. To acknowledge each person who contributed to these pages would be impossible, but here is a partial list of hosts and helpers, with our sincere gratitude.

Mark and Emily Schoenhals allowed us to use their peaceful condo in Minnesota for an extended period of research and writing while they volunteered as missionaries in Costa Rica. David Fell and his crew at Stonewood Tea in Oklahoma kept us comforted with green tea and soy lattes while we spent many hours typing sentences and fixing paragraphs. Back home in Southern California, George and the morning crew at our favorite Chick-fil-A kept us fueled for long days of writing and editing.

Our thanks to Mike and Nellie Martin for your warmth and hospitality. We so enjoy your gracious home and deeply love each member of your family. We are grateful also to Sydney Briley and her daughter Lauren. Your fireplace and candles set a perfect mood for writing and creating. Stephen and Kathie Smith, whose effective parenting we have praised in our previous books, welcomed us in rural Kansas. Bright and creative, Russ Hose sent us help and inspiration from his home in the majestic, snowy mountains of Idaho.

Lifelong friends Barry and Pam Stranz accompanied us through the deep forests of Wisconsin and the sparkling clear lakes of Minnesota while we gathered our thoughts and organized the structure of the manuscript. Good friends and mentors Brett and Mindy Rickey hosted and welcomed us in Bartow, Florida. Brett is an energetic leader and accomplished author who is working on his third book. Nearby, we were blessed by the directors and residents of the Florida Holiness Campground in Lakeland.

Rick and Vicki Power hosted us in Honolulu. Whether serving in Beijing or Texas, Kansas or Hawaii, Rick and Vicki have embraced, affirmed, and brightened our journey as authors.

Jay and Teanna Sunberg hosted us repeatedly in Sofia, Bulgaria. The lovely mountain views from their backyard and the refreshing laughter of their children are imprinted permanently in our memories. Jay and Teanna, your home is one of our favorite places on this planet.

Each of these adults and children, couples and families, contributed to the composition of this book. As writers we've learned to work anywhere, under almost any conditions, yet we highly value settings where stress is low, hospitality flows freely, and creativity flourishes. Our thanks to these friends and others for granting us places like these!

As always, much of what we know and share flows to us through the inspired teaching and godly wisdom of our home church and its senior pastors. We are forever grateful to Larry Osborne, Chris Brown, Charlie Bradshaw, Paul Savona, Gary Vanderford, J.D. Larson, and the ministers, leaders, and volunteers at North Coast Church. For more than a decade now, you've been our spiritual home. You are leading us, forming us, growing us...and we are grateful.

We are daily blessed by our parents, friends, family, and grandchildren. They keep us rooted and grounded in what really matters as we listen and serve, travel and speak, write and counsel.

Contents

Introduction 9

Part 1: The Challenge: Changing the Heart That's Mine

1. Fixing You or Finding Me? 25

2. The Hidden Danger: Unspoken Expectations 37

3. What You Don't See in Yourself: Unconscious Pride 57

4. The Power to Destroy: Unrelenting Criticism 75

5. When It's Better to Say Nothing at All: Unhelpful Gossip . . 97

6. The Elephant in the Room: Unresolved Bitterness 117

Part 2: Outcomes: When Changing Me Changes You

7. A Tale of Two Wives 139

8. Outcomes, Parts 1 and 2 167

9. Outcomes, Parts 3 and 4 181

10. Outcomes, Part 5 195

Resources 205

Introduction

L et's begin this book together by imagining that we are already close friends. We haven't seen each other for a while, but now we're meeting for coffee. After standing in line and placing our orders, we find a seat outdoors and begin catching up.

There's a lot of small talk, of course. Kids and jobs and the daily grind. We learn about your journey and you learn about ours. But after a while we're back where it all started—in a close friendship that feels even stronger now despite the passing of time. Before long we begin gently asking each other deeper questions about life.

And because of what we do as marriage counselors, we eventually ask you the same questions we ask people all over the world. They are tough questions, but isn't that what friends are for? We all need a time and place to tell trusted friends the truth about what's really going on behind closed doors. We need people whom we can trust to accept us, love us, and keep on being our friends even after we've told them deep and unpleasant truths.

So here we are, in the coffee shop, and now we're asking you, how is your marriage doing? Are you two getting closer and deeper as the years pass, or are you drifting apart? Are you two stronger because you've faced problems together, or are you weaker because stress has fractured your fragile union?

We've written this book because so many women from so many

cultures and nations have told us much the same thing. The women we meet for marriage counseling often begin by telling us about their disappointments, struggles, and setbacks. They often say to us, "This isn't what I thought marriage would be!"

So how about you? Are you living in the marriage of your dreams, or are you coping with something less, praying that things will get better someday? Like so many weary women we've met, tired of all their struggles, have you given up hope for a better relationship? Have you quietly wondered, *Is this all there is?*

Here's another way to frame the same question. How would you change your marriage today if you knew you could make a difference, if you knew you could make things better? How would you change your marriage today if you knew God's power was with you and His intention was to radically transform the structure and health of your marriage?

What can you do—all by yourself—to change or improve your marriage? What are you willing to do?

These are some of the key questions we will explore together in this book.

Maybe you're ready to move forward, even if it's all up to you. Maybe you've decided it's time to improve your marriage. You want to work, you want to learn, you want to get some wise counsel, you want to make some positive changes. You've decided that together, you and God are going to transform your marriage into the kind of relationship you know it could be, you know it should be, you know it will be. By faith you can already see it happening.

Keep your focus right there—on a bright future for your relationship. Ignore the discouraging voices and listen intently for God's counsel.

Till Death Do Us Part

Marriages have become disposable in contemporary Western culture. Many people respond to difficulties and stress in marriages in much the same way they deal with dirty diapers. When things get messy, many people simply throw away the relationship. They don't try to wash it out, clean it up, and continue working to improve it. That kind of process takes a lot of work! Instead, they discard the relationship and try on a fresh one.

Within the space of just three short generations, the West changed its attitude toward divorce. Western culture, informed by a rich tradition and heritage, once valued permanent marriages and worked to prevent divorce. Today, people in America and Europe quickly accept divorce as an option. Our society has easily adjusted to the idea that relationships are unlikely to last very long and can be disposed of. The change of attitudes is most visible among young adults as they speculate about the likelihood or even the desirability of a permanent relationship.

This cultural shift has been radically transformational. Our communities and churches are filled with fractured families and parentless children. Some people still say "till death do us part" in their wedding ceremonies, but soon afterward they start thinking, *If it's not working, I'll just start over.*

How many of your friends' marriages have lasted more than five or ten years? Not too long ago, almost all marriages did. But now people are divorcing sooner than ever before. Second and third marriages are dissolving and ending within only a few years. Many people prioritize lifelong marriage much lower than they do their personal (selfish) satisfaction.

But you have a different view of marriage and relationships. Bless you for that!

Here's a quick example of the culture we're experiencing now. A good friend of ours was recently treated to a girls' night out just before her wedding. Her circle of friends, all active churchgoers, all professing Christians, and all females in their twenties or early thirties, had this advice for our friend: "Enjoy those first 18 months or so because that's all you may get out of this. Your marriage may end before you know it!" Clearly these young adults had adjusted to the idea that marriage was likely to be a short-term experience.

If today's Christian adults have value systems like that, should we be surprised that the unchurched culture is convinced that marriages are likely to fail? If churchgoers expect marriages to be short-lived, surely those outside the community of faith have made this same adjustment and consider marriage to be fragile and disposable.

Considering the Options

In survey after survey, young adults (especially Millenials—those currently 18 to 29 years old) report that their expectations of marriage have radically lowered. Instead of saying, "When I marry, I will be with that person forever," many now say, "I may try marriage for a while, or I may not." Because marriage is considered temporary and disposable, it is easily dismissed as an unappealing option.

Increasingly, people consider marriage to be a legal and financial arrangement that makes sense for some people but is generally outmoded. "Why not just live together for a while and see if it works out?" asks Daphne, a teen we met while teaching at a marriage seminar in Eastern Europe. "I think that's the smartest approach," she told us confidently.

A lot of teens in Europe, Asia, and North America share Daphne's perspective. Many young adults begin marriage as if they were putting in a pair of disposable contact lenses. Our culture thinks marriages are temporary and easily discarded. Miracles don't happen.

The Best Choice

But our culture is wrong about that on every level—especially the part about miracles. You've picked up this book because deep within, you want to change your marriage, to work on it, to improve it…to do whatever is necessary to make your marriage better than it's ever been. You're not bound by the past. Instead, you're motivated by it. You may occasionally be discouraged by the challenges you face, but you haven't lost hope because you know in your heart that more is possible, that better days are ahead. You believe that a lifelong relationship is bound to have rough spots and that couples should expect some difficulty along the way. But you don't believe that just because life gets difficult, a marriage relationship should be thrown away!

Thank you for choosing hope over despair, for choosing to stick together rather than drift apart. You've made a choice you can live with and others can respect. You've got a lot of hard work ahead of you, but the payoff is worth it.

As marriage counselors, we deal with troubled marriages and damaged relationships every day. It's at the heart of what we do. After more than two decades of this work, we can tell you this for certain: Deciding to change your marriage instead of give up is a great first step that opens the door for God to work a miracle in your heart and in your home.

This new book is here to help you. Your husband may or may not be excited about making changes. He might be committed to working on your relationship, or he might not be willing to exert much effort. Whether your husband is ready to help or you are trying to change your marriage alone, you have plenty of reason to be encouraged today.

A lot of women in less than perfect marriages have made dramatic changes and established healthy new patterns. Many unmotivated husbands have turned around in their behaviors and attitudes because of the consistent, daily efforts of determined wives just like you.

We say this not as a matter of theory, but because of what we have seen in more than two decades of counseling marriages and families just like yours. We have also noticed that for whatever reason, the wife is usually the one who is motivated to change and improve, and she is almost always the one who takes the first steps.

We've written this book for women who want to make a difference, women who are tired of waiting for someone else to be motivated or to start working. With God's help, women just like you can experience positive and lasting changes in their marriage relationships once they begin to confidently and seriously work on making things better. We've seen it happen over and over again, across variables of race, culture, continent, age, and value systems.

Hold On to Hope

Can we promise you a miracle? No. You won't find a magic formula within these pages or a drug you can slip into your husband's morning coffee. So why talk of miracles if we can't promise you one?

Here's why: We've taken the word *hopeless* out of our vocabulary.

In more than two decades of working with some of the most troubled and difficult marriages on this small planet (including military marriages, clergy relationships, blended families, and marriages of police officers and other law enforcement professionals, ER nurses, and more), we've watched in awe as God invaded impossible situations with His grace.

Time after time, after a counseling session that ended with little or no hope, God has gently reminded us of His purposes, His power, and His ability. For God, the most difficult of human relationships present no special challenge. His power is utterly unlimited. It is also absolutely available to *you*.

So whether your marriage is moderately healthy or highly troubled, you have every reason to hold on to hope. You can partner with God as you make daily changes and create situations in which God can release His power in you, your partner, your family, and your home.

After we've finished speaking at marriage conferences or retreats, people often tell us they are excited about their decision to take *hopeless* out of their vocabulary. "That's what I want to believe too," a hurting husband may say to us. "I so desperately want to believe that," a long-suffering wife may admit.

What about you? If you have thought your situation is hopeless, are you willing to reconsider? Are you ready to allow God's grace to invade your personal space? If so, we can predict that because of your partnership with Him, dramatic change is ahead for you and the man you married.

How can we be so confident? We've watched God work before. We know what God can do and what He wants to do in marriages, and we've learned to trust Him. We've watched God make healthy relationships dramatically better. We've seen God reverse unhealthy patterns in significant ways. We've watched God revitalize dying relationships so they could go the distance—and they did.

God is not intimidated by any of the challenges you face in your marriage.

You First

When a marriage is wounded or broken, the wife almost always takes the first step to get help. Wives tend to surf the Web for the names of good counselors, ask friends for referrals, call counselors' offices, make the initial appointments, and actually show up. Husbands often walk into counseling offices reluctantly and under protest. Veteran counselors will testify that the wife and not the husband is generally the one who seems the most motivated to try to improve a good marriage or repair a broken one.

Every once in a long while, a husband initiates marriage counseling. Noting how rarely this happens, David likes to joke, "And after my coronary event, we're always glad to help out!"

If men are unlikely to stop and ask for directions while traveling, how often are they likely to ask for help with more intimate problems, including those that happen in marriage and other relationships? It just doesn't happen very often. Men are not inclined to be proactive about the relational challenges or issues they face. Instead, they often ignore or minimize their problems, responding only after serious damage has already occurred.

A man might not look for help until he experiences a cataclysmic event, such as being served with divorce papers or coming home to an empty house. Until that moment, he may not see the trouble coming, or he may believe that things have been blown out of proportion. *This is no big deal*, he will typically tell himself until it's too late. *Every marriage has its issues.*

When one of the two marriage partners initiates marriage counseling, that one person is almost always the wife. In more than two decades of experience working with couples in crisis, we have rarely watched a male take the initiative and ask for help. Men don't usually ask us for help until they're fighting a tough custody battle, trying to win their kids back, or arguing over the distribution of the couple's many debts. (These days couples don't battle over assets; they fight about who will be responsible for the credit card bills and the student loans.)

Men often wait until their wives have moved out, the house is completely empty, the kids are missing, and the bills are piling up. Then, confronted by such inescapable evidence of major problems, these men finally get motivated. Until then, most men minimize their problems, ignore the danger signs, and paddle merrily up Denial River.

Men don't see trouble coming. Somehow they notice it only after trouble has punched them in the gut a few times or perhaps knocked them down.

If it takes a village to raise a child, it often takes a cataclysmic event to raise the attention of a husband and father. By the time a man is ready to admit problems and seek help, the relationship may have deteriorated so far that the couple is already considering or actively seeking a divorce. Only then, well on their way toward a broken marriage, do most men suddenly awaken to the degree of difficulty around them.

Sometimes, the cataclysmic event appears to mark a permanent change. Even so, God may have other plans. We've learned not to trust our first impressions, and we've also learned that nothing is final regardless of how far along in the process it is.

Making the Best of a Bad Situation

For Mark and Anita, the life-changing event was history by the time they walked in our office door. They had long since given up on their relationship as husband and wife. They were tired of fighting, arguing, and getting nowhere. They had already decided to divorce. All that remained was the details.

Like many other divorcing couples, Mark and Anita approached us by telling us in their own words, "We want to have a good divorce."

Already well established on the journey to becoming legally divorced, Mark and Anita wanted the experience to be as smooth and stress free for their kids as possible. Their presenting issue was that they wanted to help their children grow up to be normal despite the end of the marriage and the breakup of the home.

By the time Mark and Anita sat down in our office, Anita had been living with her parents in another state for more than three months. She had taken the children, the pets, and most of the furniture and household belongings with her. "The children are doing pretty well overall. They've always loved their grandparents," she said. Anita's acceptance of her new situation was nearly complete.

In contrast, Mark was unable to make the mortgage payments on their home, so he was making some repairs so he could put it on the market. If the couple had any equity in the house, which was doubtful, they were hoping to split the profits equally. Meanwhile, Mark had regressed to a college-level living experience. He resided in a cramped and messy apartment with three other males, two of whom were also divorced or divorcing. Three of the four guys were also going through job changes or looking for work.

Both Mark and Anita were moving forward according to their own wisdom and counsel, and each believed that the divorce was inevitable. "I don't love her, and she doesn't love me," Mark told us succinctly. "Even the kids can see that."

Anita agreed with this analysis, through her tears. "It's been a long time since we were in love with each other," Anita said as we talked about the couple's prior history. "For as long as the kids can probably remember, all we've done is fight."

Even in their body language, the tension between Mark and Anita was tangible. Most of their recent communications were short, terse text messages about financial questions or issues with the children. They rarely spoke on the phone.

Just being together in the same place with a calm referee (counselor) was a big step. Yet Mark and Anita were not seeking help with their relationship. That was over.

Mark and Anita had reached a seemingly logical conclusion: Because they showed no signs of love and their children were constantly hearing them argue and fight, the logical move was to split up, figure out the financial issues, and begin to build new lives for themselves.

"We get along better now that we're not living together," Anita confided during an early session with us. "So maybe this is meant to be."

Mark and Anita's deepest fear was that their divorce would somehow harm or damage their children. Could this be prevented by good planning? Was there a way they could prepare the kids to get through the divorce and have as normal a life as possible?

"Both of us love our kids," Mark said emphatically. "Even though we don't love each other anymore, both of us do love our kids. I know Anita wants the best for them, and I know I do too. So please tell us how we can handle this whole divorce thing so that our kids turn out okay."

Deciding that they had been unlucky in marriage, Mark and Anita still wanted to be effective as parents despite their divorce. This attitude was commendable, but we didn't give up on Mark and Anita's relationship simply because they had done so. Frankly, we wanted to see what God's opinion might be.

Rewriting History

Fast forward to now.

Mark and Anita are living together cooperatively and peacefully in their original home. Mark has completed many of the repair projects and hopes to get the rest of the work finished soon. The kids have returned to their school districts and play with their old friends. The couple has cancelled divorce plans. "Sometimes we can't believe we actually went through all that," Anita says.

Mark and Anita remain in counseling to improve their relationship, not to work through a divorce. If you catch a glimpse of them at Walmart or sitting in the bleachers for a high school football game, you may see them holding hands or smiling at each other. People looking in from the outside, not knowing the couple's history, would naturally assume that Mark and Anita are a happily married couple, and they'd be right. Mark and Anita love each other, support each other, and are committed to each other for life.

A Place to Run To

Today, Mark and Anita are active in a progressive church in their community. During the divorce planning, both had stopped attending their church, though Anita occasionally took the kids to her parents' small country church. "I wasn't so sure about God anymore," Mark confides. "I mean, where was He when all that stuff was happening to us? I kind of quit believing for a while."

Couples who are divorcing tend to run away from the church and not toward it. Many congregations who support marriages and have resources for married couples have been slow to include divorce care and divorce recovery among their core ministries. To engage today's culture, the church must realistically assess people's situations, reach out in compassion, and develop resources to be helpful.

Churches send this message to married couples: "We care about you, and we've got programs for you." The unspoken but perceived message to divorced people is often different: "You may not fit in here because we don't believe in divorce."

This may not be the message that churches intend to send. While actively supporting and encouraging marriage, churches need to do a much better job of including divorced adults in their services, small groups, and other programs. Churches need to come alongside stepfamilies and blended families with effective training in parenting, conflict resolution, and more.

Over and Above

Meanwhile, fighting is rare these days in Mark and Anita's home. Both adults have learned to watch for the signs that relational trouble may be brewing. "We stop ourselves before it goes that far," Anita explains. "That way we don't end up saying or doing things we don't mean. It's a real change in how we relate to each other!"

We say this carefully, and yet it's true. In a relatively short time, Mark and Anita have quit saying, "We just want to help our kids get through this divorce okay," and they now enjoy a healthier marriage than do many of the couples we see in church pews or at weekend soccer games. God invaded and saved this marriage, and He put it on a pathway toward health and growth, giving the couple brand-new tools for understanding each other, communicating better, and sharing the decision-making process.

Mark and Anita's marriage had seemed to be over, but now it's over and above the average marriage. And this happened not because they wanted a good marriage but as an unplanned consequence of trying to have a good divorce!

God often does amazing things in situations like these.

A Two-Step Process

Mark and Anita are a living true story with a great chapter ending. But what matters here is that their relationship shows us a process that we frequently observe as we watch God work to heal hurting marriages. The process begins with a genuine heart change in one partner. Gradually, as the honesty and intensity of that heart change becomes visible to the other partner, the other partner also begins to experience a change of heart, perhaps slowly at first. Finally, as God's grace invades the strongholds and fortresses of hurting hearts, both partners experience radical and lasting change.

Most of us don't realize that when we begin to struggle in key relationships such as a marriage, we erect some strong walls around our hearts to protect ourselves from getting hurt. This is a natural human tendency and is not inherently evil. Yet as things move forward, we end up relating to our life partners from behind our strong walls of protection. We quit being vulnerable and transparent. (For a further discussion of vulnerability and transparency, you might enjoy reading our recent book *The Soul-Mate Marriage: The Spiritual Journey of Becoming One.*)

Subtly at first and then much more visibly, we begin to relate to our partners from behind our well-defended walls. Our conversations with them are not tender or broken or open. We've decided that to be open isn't safe, and being tender means being hurt. Gradually a hard shell forms around our deepest emotions, and our interactions become formal, distant, and even businesslike. We speak with our spouses as if we were at war and negotiating a treaty.

We may love our partners, but this love is not visible in tenderness, in openness, in vulnerability, or in other patterns of healthy courtship and intimacy. Instead, our defensive habits reveal a muted hostility that withdraws, waits, and often even prays for change—in the other person. Yet when meaningful change does happen, it often begins in us, not in our partner.

That process—meaningful change in our own hearts and then miracles and God's power at work in our partners—is what we'll explore together in these pages.

What about your personal journey? Is your own marriage as far down the road to divorce as Mark and Anita had traveled? Have you thought about it, talked about it, or perhaps even done some planning for it? Has one of you already resigned to the idea that your marriage is over, that it has no future, that the only realistic and reasonable outcome is a divorce? Are you searching for a process that is as amicable as possible in order to spare the kids and work out a reasonably agreeable settlement?

If so, be warned—God may have other ideas. He may begin changing your marriage by changing your own heart and life. He may already be at work to bring you hope and a future. God is like that.

Speaking of your future, it's the entire reason that we wrote this book. We want you to know that there is hope ahead and that better days are possible.

This hope has at least two parts: genuine change and spiritual growth in your own life, and then, by God's grace, authentic transformation in your partner. This hope applies to marriages that are mostly okay and to marriages that have been without joy and affection for a long time.

Before you decide to give up on your marriage, give God a chance to work. Let Him begin His work in your own heart (which is where our book opens as well) and then watch as He powerfully stirs the heart, mind, attitudes, and behavior of the man you married. The change in your husband will be God's work, not yours, yet God's power will be released and made potent through the changes in you.

If you're willing to open yourself to God's insight and wisdom, if you choose to accept God's counsel about your own motives and behavior, and if you're hoping to watch God move in your relationship even if it seems hopeless and futile, then you are exactly the reader for whom we wrote this book.

For more than two decades now, we've watched God intervene—against all odds and in seemingly impossible situations—to bring His hope and His healing. We are praying that as you read these few pages, you'll allow God to be who He is and to do what He does best.

Part I

THE CHALLENGE:
Changing the Heart That's Mine

Fixing You or Finding Me?

Take a moment to look again at this book's front cover and title. Did you notice that we chose not to promise a quick fix or ten easy steps? Our mission as marriage counselors is to help you move forward toward becoming the best woman and wife you can possibly be. Along the way, we'll show you how the choices you make can affect your own life as well as your partner's, and we'll give you real-life examples of how God is working in marriages like yours.

You won't find a weapon for attacking your husband or a strategy for manipulating his behavior. We don't offer new ideas for leverage so you can win a never-ending battle between the sexes. We believe war is highly overrated anyway. We really start cheering when peace breaks out around the kitchen table or in the bedroom.

So, what if peace breaks out in your marriage? And if peace is going to break out in your home, how might it begin? More to the point, with whom might it begin?

We hope you'll pray, *Please, Lord, let peace begin with me*. If that's the approach you're taking, you'll find help and healing in these pages as well as a lot of practical, immediately useful advice. The help you'll find here comes from our experience with hundreds of other wives who have traveled this road before you.

Of course, your man is mentioned in this book's title also, and we'll explore together how husbands can and do change their unhelpful behaviors. Change happens! But the change in *you* and your behavior is most likely to precipitate a change in him and his behavior. That's not a formula or a secret recipe. It's simply an observation based on how God has worked in the lives of His children throughout history. It's the way Scripture describes the dynamic effectiveness of a godly wife as she transforms her marriage relationship in helpful and positive directions.

Regardless of what some advertisers may promise, changes like these don't happen easily, quickly, or without effort. But let's face it, is life really that simple? Does *any* major change happen overnight and without hard work? Can we lose weight, manage other people's behaviors, or become wealthy quickly and without much effort? Real life rarely yields its complexity to simple answers.

Many wives tend to think their husbands need to change, their kids need to adjust their attitudes, or the problem people in their families are the ones who need a lesson in humility. How easy it is to look around our world and notice all the issues and all the problems that other people have—which really do need to be changed by cooperation with God's grace.

Wouldn't it be great if we could magically transform everyone around us who seems to need a makeover? Yes, a lot of people appear to need that. That firmly stubborn and frequently critical supervisor on our job could use a "kinder and gentler" redo. That nosy neighbor who refuses to mind her own business, always looking for new tidbits of spicy gossip around the neighborhood? Bam—let's turn her into a kindly-tongued Christian today.

An old spiritual includes the line, "Not my brother, not my sister, but it's me, O Lord, standin' in the need of prayer." It's a great line with an important focus. Instead of worrying about the issues of the people who work beside me at the office or live in my home, I can sing these lyrics and open my heart to what God wants to do within me—renew and change my attitudes, behaviors, and choices.

That song frames our approach as we write these pages. This book is not a magnifying glass to help you find the faults of others. Instead, it's more like a mirror to look into so you can examine yourself. And as we open this book together, we're going to begin by looking straight into that mirror, with God standing beside us, so we get an accurate and clear reflection of our own image, with God's help.

There's no need to be afraid of this process. The God who stands beside us loves us and wants to help us and move us forward. God is not like a misguided earthly parent, always finding fault with whatever we do because it's not good enough. Instead, God is our own heavenly Father, an encourager who believes in us, is proud of us, and stands ready to help us accomplish more and better things.

As we look into a mirror and examine our hearts, we'll uncover our true motives and reveal our frequently unhelpful perspectives. We'll discover that other wives have confronted these same issues before us. Other women have confessed their sins, repented of their hard hearts, and been changed by God's grace. Other marriages have made stunning progress because someone was obedient. Often, that someone was a woman just like you.

When a woman experiences a strong movement of God in her own heart, her resulting transformation often leads to an equal reaction elsewhere. Her husband begins to change also. Yet regardless of whether your husband ever changes, the payoff in this book is even closer to home. It happens within you.

The stories, concepts, ideas, and Scriptures in these pages have the power to help you become your best self ever, the woman you always dreamed of being. That woman is busy going God's direction and being God's kind of person in her interactions with the network of people all around her. That woman has the motives, the attitudes, the speech patterns, and the behavior choices that God has shown her are wisest and best. In the midst of a hurting neighborhood and society, that woman is a healer and a helper to all who know her. She is making a difference.

That woman, with God's help, can be you.

We will move confidently in that direction, learning a lot as we go about becoming our husbands' best friends. But the bottom line of this little book is not about our husbands. It's really about us. The primary goal and purpose that we seek in these few pages is clearly reinforced by the chorus of that same old spiritual: "It's me, it's me, it's me, O Lord, standin' in the need of prayer."

A Scriptural Perspective

In the pages that follow, we'll frame our approach around the key biblical principle of the moat and the beam (King James Version) or the log and the speck (Good News Translation). This biblical understanding will provide us with the foundation for everything we talk about between the covers of this book.

Do you remember this particular teaching example that Jesus provided to His disciples? You can find it in Matthew 7:1-5. Here's how it reads in the Good News Translation.

> Do not judge others, so that God will not judge you, for God will judge you in the same way you judge others, and he will apply to you the same rules you apply to others. Why, then, do you look at the speck in your brother's eye and pay no attention to the log in your own eye? How dare you say to your brother, "Please let me take that speck out of your eye," when you have a log in your own eye? You hypocrite! First take the log out of your own eye, and then you will be able to see clearly to take the speck out of your brother's eye.

Jesus's teaching is sharp and insightful, and it gets right to the point. Before we go rushing off to fix and repair other people, maybe we should spend some time working on our own problems.

Looking in the Wrong Direction

Jesus understands our human nature very well. In this passage He addresses the way we easily notice the faults and the failings of the people around us. Meanwhile, we have far worse faults and much bigger issues that we ought to be seriously working on. But instead of working out our own problems and getting ourselves in better shape, we point our fingers at the people around us, highlighting their issues, their needs, their flaws.

"My goodness," we say as we notice someone else's fault or failure, "that person sure needs a lot of help!" Luckily for that person, we've noticed the problem, and we're ready to get to work helping him or her improve and change. Meanwhile, we tend to ignore or rationalize our own blind spots, downplaying the importance or scope of our own shortcomings. We see other people's sins and are ready to point them out, criticizing the other people and worrying about how to fix them. We develop strategies for how someone else can get better. Often, we share these ideas with others: "Here's what Sally needs to understand…"

Somehow we don't notice our own bigotry or self-righteous pride. We minimize our own jealousy or bitterness while noticing even the smallest things that our friends or family members need to work on in their own lives. We get focused on changing the smaller issues in the people around us. Instead, we ought to be working on the larger issues where we ourselves struggle and need God's help.

Apparently this is a universal human condition, which is why it occurs within so many marriage relationships also. This powerful teaching of Jesus applies to all of us today, and it especially applies to wives and husbands who are learning how to live together and adjust to each other in love.

The View from Up Close

Forming a united and long-lasting relationship takes a lot of work, and we usually tend to pay special attention to the work our partners need to do. We're busy raising our children and managing a household. We're working part-time or full-time outside the home, but every night we pull into our driveway and confront a whole world of work to do under our own roof. No one else has done it! No one else seems to be trying! *Can I get some help around here?*

Women around the world feel this way, and they voice their

feelings to David and me during counseling sessions, retreats, and conferences. Their emotions are normal and valid but not always particularly helpful. Here's why.

When we're doing most of the household work ourselves, we get frustrated, and our frustration seems entirely valid. No wonder we feel this way. *Just look around the place!* Our righteous anger comes as no surprise. *Can't you see what simple justice would require here?* We're right and we know it. And before long, we become so convinced of our own rightness that we quit working on the things we can truly change: our own thoughts, feelings, words, and actions.

Instead of doing helpful and useful things, we begin to form harmful habits. We begin to see ourselves as noble and moral and spiritual. We start seeing others as falling short, lacking in spiritual depth, or devoid of character.

When you are married to someone, you are in a unique position to observe his faults and shortcomings. Others may not easily or often recognize these problems in your partner, but you have an up-close and personal view of what's wrong with him. Until you began sharing a home, these issues may not have been visible. But now, sometimes they are all you can think about. You're focused on changing the person you live with because after all, he really needs to be changed! No one can see that better than you.

So you get to work, devising all sorts of plans that will adjust, improve, transform, and enlighten your life partner. Luckily for him, he married someone who has the wisdom and understanding to lead him through all these important transformations. If only you can get him to listen to you, he'll become superhusband right away. He'll see and understand how he needs to change, and he'll get busy doing it.

If he doesn't get started quickly, you'll be right there to remind him again and again. And if all else fails, you can drag him off to a counselor who is certain to take your side and rule in favor of justice: "Husband, change thyself!"

This is exactly why many women eventually drag their husbands into counselors' offices. It's the last great hope of fairness. Once the evidence has been clearly gathered and effectively presented, surely the counselor will rule in favor of the wife. So if all else fails, let's get some counseling!

But how well does this strategy work? Have you ever noticed how rarely your husband gets excited about marriage counseling with your minister or priest? Husbands intuitively understand that as soon as the counselor's door swings shut and the session begins, their day in court is at hand. They fear they'll be found guilty, so they'd rather not show up.

Many husbands would rather visit the dentist than see a counselor. At the dentist's office, their pain is short-lived and can perhaps be relieved with medication. But after they see a counselor, Novocain doesn't help.

Motivated wives and uncooperative husbands are the daily bread and butter of marriage counselors. And without some genuinely effective biblical counseling, many wives are likely to believe that they are right and their husbands are wrong. Wives often hope that in the counseling office, justice will be served and their husbands will be told to change their behavior. These women believe that the solution to their problems is for their husbands to change.

Is that what you often believe?

Time for a Focus Adjustment

Then Jesus comes along and helps us adjust our focus. "Why are you worrying about all those little issues in your life partner? Instead, why don't you look at your own heart and life? If you do, you'll notice that you have larger and more serious flaws that need your full and complete attention before you focus on trying to change someone else."

It's amazing how Jesus nails it with just one metaphor.

The problem is this: We're in a hurry to fix and repair our husbands when God in His wisdom would rather begin by fixing us.

Sometimes the husband isn't the only one who dreads counseling. Often the wife does as well. She's tired of yelling and nagging and describing the problem, and she's ready for a referee who will step into the ring, blow a whistle, and declare her the winner of the fight. But she's not prepared for a counselor who blows a whistle, sends her back to her own corner, and tells her to get to work on her own problems.

Time out! When did this become all about me?

None of Us Are Without Sin

Jesus introduces a very similar concept in another setting. While He is teaching in the temple, the religious elite and political power-brokers bring him a woman who has been caught in the very act of adultery. The Jewish law is quite clear and specific: The penalty for her sin is death by stoning. "Here is what the law says," the high priests and self-righteous religious leaders remind Jesus in case He's forgotten. "Now, what do You say?"

Scripture makes it clear that the priests and leaders are hoping that Jesus will incriminate Himself also. They've heard that He is gentle and kind, so they're hoping He will disregard the law and say something compassionate and caring. "Aw, never mind the law. Just let the poor woman go with a warning. I'm sure it won't happen again." Then they could accuse Jesus of breaking the law and condoning the woman's sin.

But the leaders are outclassed in a moment. Steadily writing in the dirt, Jesus avoids their clever arguments in a surprising way.

"Hey," Jesus says after a time of reflection. "Let's go ahead and stone her, just like the law requires. And here's an idea. Why don't we all line up to throw the rocks at her? Those of you who are perfect and without sin, why don't you get right on up in the front of the line? All right, let's get started!"

Jesus doesn't break the law. He upholds the highest moral and ethical standard. If we're going to punish someone else, Jesus suggests here, why don't we let the perfect people begin the punishing? That approach seems fair and right, doesn't it? To let the perfect people take their vengeance first seems to be the reasonable thing to do. Ready to line up and get busy, perfect people?

To their eventual credit, the duplicitous and self-righteous religious leaders figure out one key truth: None of them are perfect. Accordingly, they are unable to follow Jesus's suggestion. Not a single one of them deserves to cast the first stone. None of the woman's accusers are perfect.

They file out of the room, one by one, beginning with the older ones. Eventually the room contains only Jesus and the guilty woman.

Then the only one who is actually qualified to cast the first stone—the world's only perfect person—looks at this woman, perhaps for the first time. "Woman," He asks gently, "Where are those who accuse you?"

"They are all gone," she tells Him. "There is no one here to condemn me."

"I don't condemn you either," Jesus explains to her. "Now, leave your sin in the past. Go and begin living a life that pleases God."

Jesus makes the same offer to each one of us, one sinner at a time.

Traps and Pitfalls of the Frustrated Wife

As we work with marriages around the globe, certain patterns become clearly visible in relationships. After more than two decades of working with couples, we've seen universal principles at work in many homes and many marriages. These patterns affect the dynamics of husband-wife relationships in cities and villages, in rural and urban communities, in developed nations and primitive tribes. The challenges of marriage and family are much the same for all of us regardless of which country we call home.

When we wives are in the right and know it, we tend to behave in ways that are hugely unhelpful. As we'll see in the next few chapters, these behaviors fit into five broad patterns. Although a wife's motives may be good, and although to her credit she may be the one who most wants to improve and strengthen the relationship, if she behaves in one of these five patterns, she is probably harming her marriage even while believing she's helping it. These patterns are not only self-defeating but also capable of destroying the home and family.

We are not trying to frame a new theology of sin or a new understanding of grace. We know what we don't know: We are not theologians, and we won't pretend to unpack a doctrine of sin in this short volume. We also aren't trying to point blame at one partner in a marriage. We're simply pointing out that when wives begin working on their own issues, meaningful change occurs.

We're using the terms *traps* and *pitfalls* to help all of us learn how to avoid some of the common mistakes people make in their key relationships. We hope to catch your attention and to underscore the fact that these patterns are not merely unhelpful and wrong—they are often massively destructive to a person and a relationship. Falling into these patterns can be easy and seem normal, but it can also destroy your marriage one moment or interaction at a time until the relationship crashes and perhaps ends.

If you are frustrated by your husband's behaviors or attitudes, agonizing over his apparent lack of interest in making the relationship work, you may find yourself in these next few chapters. In fact, you may find yourself more than once. Many wives exhibit two or three of these patterns at the same time. In general, the greater the number of unhelpful patterns present in a home, the sooner the negative outcomes will arrive.

Sadly, we see these patterns rising up time and time again in the behaviors of active churchgoers and passionate worshippers. The best women can and often do act out in the worst possible ways in the confines of their own homes. They may mean well, but they behave badly. Meanwhile, they honestly believe that their husbands need help and that they (the wives) are the godly ones.

These traps, pitfalls, or patterns of behavior tend to corrode or wear down relationships instead of building the trust, intimacy, and committed partnership you so deeply desire. Falling into these traps and pitfalls is so easy and so normal that many wives find themselves caught in them before they realize what has happened.

Does this sound like anyone you know? Does it sound like the person in your mirror?

Wouldn't it feel great to start moving forward in helpful ways, finding healthy habits of relating to and understanding your husband? We'll show you how to do it, but first it's time to spend some time in front of your mirror, looking at five ways wives can get tripped up by their own words, thoughts, and deeds as they cope with husbands who can't or won't work to improve a marriage.

When a wife is struggling with an uncooperative or uncommunicative husband, when her life partner doesn't seem to be pulling his own load or doing his own share, we can sympathize with her task. We cheer for her. But as we cheer, we also realize that she is under a lot of pressure and is vulnerable to several traps and pitfalls. There are some serious missteps that might keep her from achieving the one thing she is working so hard to achieve—a better marriage.

What if you wanted a better marriage and were ready to go to work, but you also knew in advance how to avoid these traps and pitfalls? What if you could learn from the real-life experiences of other wives, avoid their mistakes, and learn from their accomplishments and successes?

Other wives have faced the same challenges you do. Their stories are here, and these accounts will probably remind you a lot of the situations you're facing right now.

Be encouraged today. You and God can do this, and you'll be amazed at the results.

The Hidden Danger: Unspoken Expectations

Light snow begins to fall as we commute along I-435 in the Kansas City metro area. It's early December, the first weekend after the busy Thanksgiving holiday. We are meeting with a couple for dinner this evening to interview them for this book. We left our hotel a bit early so we can drive the scenic route toward one of our favorite places in the U.S.—the Country Club Plaza district.

We're in a rented Civic, rounding one of many sweeping bends along the interstate, when the first few flakes of snow begin to float silently across our car's windshield. Both of us immediately exclaim the blatantly obvious, beaming like children: "It's snowing!" We can't quit smiling as the fat white flakes begin to cluster on the hood of our charcoal gray Honda. This isn't a storm or a blizzard; it's merely a dusting of beautiful crystals. Tomorrow morning, the shrubs and trees of Kansas City will glisten with bright and chilly natural ornaments. I can't wait to see it.

When you live in Southern California, snow is an exotic rarity, the kind of thing you treasure and celebrate. It isn't the traffic hazard or the noxious annoyance it might be in Buffalo or Bozeman during a long dark season of cold days and freezing nights. Instead, it's a reason to pause and glance skyward, to drink in the moment and savor the experience.

I (Lisa) grew up in Minnesota, so snow reminds me of family traditions and childhood memories. Somehow my mind manages to block out the stalled cars, the hours of shoveling driveways and sidewalks, the canceled events, and other adversities for which snow was often responsible. Instead, I tend to remember ice skating in the park, making snow angels on the lawn, or riding in the way-back seat of our Rambler wagon as we drove out to Grandma's farm for a winter holiday.

Snow brings out the happy in me.

David switches off the radio and slows the Civic to a measured pace. Both of us stare at the gathering cluster of gleaming snowflakes as we ride along in silent admiration of God's choice of weather. This is winter's version of smelling the roses—we're taking the time to admire the icy white sprinkles.

These days, both of us love winter, but we prefer to visit it from a distance rather than build an igloo and reside there. Earlier in our marriage we lived in Vancouver and Minneapolis. In both of those places, snow is more common and less welcome. After completing our tour of duty in winter's strongholds, we have moved relentlessly toward frothy blue waves, sandy beaches, and glowing sunsets.

Today, as full-time authors and frequent speakers, we make our home in a place where sunshine is reliable, ocean breezes are refreshing, and flowering plants crowd every season of the year with fresh blooms and colorful displays. San Diego manages to pause indefinitely on the border between spring and summer, balancing there for about 360 days of the year. Sometimes a few more.

So on this night, as tourists visiting winter, we gaze at the snow in admiration and celebration. Soon, as we dine on the Country Club Plaza, the dazzling flakes will be silhouetted against thousands of colored lights in one of the prettiest urban places on earth. Neither of us can quit smiling.

Not Compatible but Oh So Committed

Later tonight we will meet a couple that eHarmony would never have connected. Their profiles would have passed by each other on the company's servers, never stopping to notice each other's data.

Brent and Carrie have been married for 18 years. Not just your average couple, they are enjoying a happy and thriving relationship. Still, people who meet and get to know them can't quite imagine how they got together. They are radically different from one another. They have different temperaments, different perspectives, and much different interests. How did they find each other? Why does their relationship work? Their union makes no sense by any standard of compatibility.

"If I had been their premarital counselor, I wouldn't have encouraged their relationship," David admits on our way to dinner. "Their differences are too great, and their similarities are too few. I can see how they might be attracted to each other, but I can't see how they'd manage to bond and adhere or go the distance. I never would have encouraged them toward marriage."

I agree, thinking of the many conversations I've had with Carrie over the course of our two-decade friendship. She's so unlike her husband, I can't quite figure out why they chose each other. I've heard the story of their courtship a dozen times or more, but I'm looking forward to hearing it again tonight. I need to be reminded of how these two found each other. I also want to hear again why and how they stayed together when their marriage seemed poised to crash and burn at any moment.

Apparently, it almost did.

Driving in a slow motorcade of evening traffic along the wide expanse of Ward Parkway, David and I are more than happy when frequent red lights stop us at picturesque, tree-lined intersections. Beside us in each lane, SUVs and minivans are packed with children staring out their car windows with glee, entranced by the fat flakes and the multicolored lights.

For several blocks along the parkway, nearly every house is lit up with bright strands of lights strung from trees to roofs and even to neighbors' homes. We're early for our dinner appointment, so we veer

slightly off Ward Parkway and roll very slowly through this neighborhood's lovely holiday display.

"It's even better than last year," David says softly as we admire the
anchor block of the neighborhood. I concur.

We pause the Honda in front of a home that is broadcasting
Christmas carols through outdoor speakers. I crack my car window
ever so slightly, improving the sound without letting too much warm
air escape. David and I sit in silence, listening to "Joy to the World"
in near-perfect fidelity.

The hymn celebrates the arrival of our Savior, born to a world
that should have been expecting Him yet somehow got distracted
and missed the moment.

Moments to Remember

As we enter the Country Club Plaza, a shopping and dining paradise that was modeled after Seville, Spain, David slides down all our
electric windows, cranks up the car's heater, and rolls slowly and quietly through streets adorned with Mediterranean-themed buildings,
each outlined in various colors of holiday lighting.

Beside us, a horse-drawn carriage rolls by, bells clinking as two
couples huddle together for warmth under bright red blankets. In
front of us, intrepid pedestrians dash across the street toward the
jewelry store. Are they shopping for rings? Are they getting engaged
this holiday season?

Years ago, I bought the fabric for my wedding dress at Kaplan's
here on the Plaza. (Never again have I spent that much money on
a single purchase of fabric!) The Country Club Plaza is a romantic
and inviting environment for David and me.

Our Honda rolls quietly toward our dinner date at Houston's,
and as we get close to the restaurant, David pulls into a covered parking garage. "The snow is beautiful, but the roof is helpful," my husband observes, morphing one of our frequently quoted movie lines
into a winter joke. Only the two of us would get it.

The couple we're meeting runs late, which is true to their usual form. By the time they arrive we've sipped a few cups of coffee, gotten to know our server (she's a grad student in educational psychology at nearby University of Missouri–Kansas City), and greeted someone we knew as we entered the restaurant. We're relaxed and at ease, ready for an evening that will be part interview, part counseling session, and all enjoyable.

"You knew we'd be late, didn't you?" Carrie asks us about 17 minutes overdue. She's grinning broadly as she interrogates us. "You were expecting that from us, right?" David and I look at each other sheepishly, without comment. How do you answer a question like that? With guilty smiles, we say yes.

Brent slides into our booth with a larger-than-life gesture. "Traffic…" he says broadly, shrugging his shoulders. "It's always horrible at this time of year, but what can you do?"

I look at my husband, stifling a laugh. I can read David's mind as he mentally answers the rhetorical question. *Well, you might try leaving early.* He winks at me, catching me in the act of reading his thoughts.

We laugh our way through appetizers and a round of Diet Cokes. Does our generation have its own signature beverage? I look around the table. We are four middle-aged adults, and each of us orders diet colas instead of regular. When did we cross over? When did we quit living dangerously and stop drinking full-bore sugar with every meal? Ah, to be 25 again, sipping a regular cola and feeling immortal.

David leads us toward our topic for the evening. "Let's not start at the beginning," he suggests. "Let's start at the point where both of you thought the marriage was over. What was going on at that time, and how did you manage to get through all that? Why are you still married today? Better yet, why are you so happily married today?"

David pauses from his questions and explains what he's thinking. "If anyone ever reads this book of ours, that's what they'll want to know. How did you go from crash to crush, from burn to learn?"

He can turn a phrase, this man I married. Let the interview begin.

Marriage, Interrupted

Brent jumps in without further invitation. "I was completely surprised. I thought we had a pretty good marriage," he begins. "I didn't know anything was wrong. I was working a lot, which is normal for me, and every day I came home to a wife and two little kids who seemed to love me. So if there were danger signs or warning signals, I sure missed them."

He is gregarious, outgoing...a life-of-the-party type who makes friends instantly and connects with almost anyone. He's also an outrageous flirt, dialing up the charm for the females and switching it back down for the males. Surrounded by the good ol' boys, he's all man, the alpha male, the big dog in a crowd of big-dog wannabes.

Everyone loves him. But early in their marriage relationship, "everyone" did not include his wife. "It was our fifth anniversary," Carrie recalls, "but he didn't remember. I cooked dinner, and as usual, Brent was late getting home. He didn't bring me a card or a present. I don't know why that surprised me; he hadn't brought me a card or a gift for any of our other anniversaries. Forgetting our special days was entirely normal and completely typical for him.

"But that night, it suddenly all snapped. I found myself hoping that for the first time, my husband would burst through that front door on time with a big smile on his face, hiding a fresh bouquet of long-stemmed roses behind his back. I longed for all those silly clichés—fresh flowers, a box of truffles or chocolates, maybe a bottle of my favorite perfume. I built up all these hopes in my head despite a mountain of evidence that things like that would never happen for us.

"That night, I desperately wanted my ideal husband to walk through the door and romance me. But instead, my actual husband walked in the door, grabbed one of our sons, and started throwing him up in the air. Before I knew it, the whole room was in chaos, Brent was playing with both kids, and I was completely ignored.

"A happy anniversary? Not exactly.

"Finally he spoke to me. 'What's for dinner?' He didn't even look at me. He was bouncing Hudson up and down, playing rough with both of our little boys. I almost hit him with something right then and there. But instead, I gave him the drop-dead stare to end all drop-dead stares."

She pauses in her story, remembering.

"I can tell you exactly what I was thinking. *Why on earth did I marry this complete idiot who can't even remember his own anniversary? Why on earth did I have children with a man who doesn't even romance me the way other husbands do their wives on their anniversaries?*

"I had a case of it," Carrie admits over refills of our diet colas. I notice that our server is spending a fair amount of time near our table, intent on overhearing as much of our conversation as she can. And I can't blame her. The quick pleasantries are out of the way, and we're getting into it now.

Carrie and I take a bathroom break together.

"Am I talking too much?" she asks. "We worked through all this stuff and resolved it a long time ago. But when I talk about it now, I can still feel all those same feelings. I can still capture those same emotions."

We talk together, just us women, deciding it's okay in this environment to go ahead and reveal how she was actually feeling back at that time. "I think we're both okay, I really do," she says. "I just wouldn't want to start anything that difficult all over again."

After our restroom break we return to the table, and Carrie picks up the narrative where she left off. She can't even talk about it without sighing and sagging. Her body language, whether she knows it or not, reveals that this issue deeply weighed on her and challenged her ability to rise above it and keep pushing forward.

"I felt trapped at home, caring for two little boys we hadn't really planned on," she begins. "I felt stuck in a boring domestic life I never wanted while my husband wined and dined his way to success in business. I was getting older and looking older and feeling older, wishing I had stayed in school and pursued my master's degree before I started hatching babies every eighteen months.

"It was so completely unfair. My husband dressed well and spent tons of money on his clothes. He jumped into our new car and drove off, spending thirty dollars or more treating prospective customers to business lunches. He was living the life he dreamed of while I was trapped in a nightmare at home, eating leftovers and dreaming of a much different life.

"There were days when I loved holding my boys on my lap, when I felt successful as a homemaker, and when it was almost enough for me, but those days were pretty rare at that point. Most of the time I smelled the dirty diapers, washed the dirty dishes, and ran my husband's expensive suits to the dry cleaners while wishing for something more. I felt sorry for myself, and as far as I could tell I had good reason to.

"My husband was carefree and had a happy and easy life. I was trapped at home with poop to clean up, yelling back and forth with my kids all day. I wondered how this had happened to me. I wanted to get my master's degree in English literature, but every dirty diaper seemed to mock my dreams, reminding me that I was trapped and that all the things I hoped for were never going to happen."

She pauses in what has become a lengthy monologue.

"So like I said, it was our fifth anniversary," she says softly, remembering the night. "For me, that's the night I was ready to walk out and start over somewhere else."

Not the End, but the Beginning

Brent looks at us to make sure we're getting all this and then briefly reiterates his perspective. "I was clueless," he shrugs. "I had no idea Carrie was feeling or thinking these things. I thought we had a pretty good, pretty normal marriage going on."

Even though we're talking about times that are long since passed, and even though Brent and Carrie have moved on, grown together, and built an intimate friendship, these are not happy memories, and the emotions are still raw at times. It's time for a joke, and we all sense it. As usual, Brent provides the humor.

"But you do have to admit," he tells us all broadly, with a sweep of his hand across the whole expanse of our booth, "if anybody can make clueless look good, I can!" He gives us a cheesy grin and a handsome pose, and we all laugh. Thanks, guy. We needed that.

Clueless Brent believed he was living in a pretty good marriage. He believed his home life was normal and acceptable. As far as he knew, his wife loved him. They had sex, didn't they? And it was pretty good sex, wasn't it? He had produced two strapping young boys already.

Yes, a pretty good marriage. One wife, two sons, a nice car in the driveway, and a salary that was growing every year, thanks to commissions and bonus payments. A born sales professional, Brent was earning a high five-figure income and looking forward to more.

Okay, the kids could be a little much at times. *But let's face it, boys will be boys,* he told himself. As Brent reviewed his own life in those days, he mostly felt successful, reasonably happy, and loved at home.

Meanwhile, his wife felt trapped, frustrated, and unfulfilled. By her own accounts she was ready to leave him and start over, even if she had to drag the two kids along with her. She figured she could find a sitter and relaunch her educational career. Anything would be better than spending another day with an inconsiderate man who ignored her needs, indulged his own wishes, and spent more on toys and recreation than she spent on groceries and the daily needs of the household.

How can two people be living such separate realities in the same home? How can one husband be so completely clueless about his wife's feelings and needs? Here's the answer in just two words: unspoken expectations.

Unspoken expectations form the basis of one of the easiest traps couples can fall into, especially when they rush into marriage on a hormone high, unified by affection and a taste for freedom, without going through the slow but always helpful process of seeking wise counsel and verifying their compatibility.

Many couples see marriage as a way to start a new life and to finally be free of parents, siblings, roommates, or other baggage that emerging adults are ready to be rid of.

We'll finally have a place of our own, Brent remembers thinking in the days approaching his marriage. *We'll have our own life; we'll be free to do things the way we want to, not the way our families want us to.* For Brent, it was all about the freedom of having his own place, being his own boss, and making his own choices…plus the added advantage of having a cook and housekeeper nearby.

Meanwhile, Carrie was dreaming of a romantic, attentive husband who would live up to her unspoken expectations. An avid reader and a frequent renter of chick flicks, Carrie entered marriage with strong opinions about what it would be like and how her husband would behave.

"My dad gave my mom handwritten cards on every major occasion," she recalls later. "I thought that was so special and so thoughtful. Instead of just buying a card, he put a lot of thought into what he wanted to say. Sometimes he wrote really corny poetry, but my mom would always cry and hug him. All of us knew Daddy loved her.

"Sometimes he came home with random gifts for Mom for no special reason," Carrie remembers today. "From the grin on his face, we'd know he'd picked up something for her. Maybe he'd stopped and picked some flowers, or maybe he'd brought her an album or a book. Sometimes it was as simple as her favorite candy bar—in those days maybe a twenty-five-cent expense. But it wasn't the price that mattered. It was the fact that Daddy constantly, consistently, attentively told my mom that he loved her, that she was special, that she was the queen of his heart."

Not unreasonably, this prospective bride expected her future husband to follow her father's pattern of romancing and wooing his wife. She didn't realize her father was more attentive than the average guy. In her view, husbands wooed their wives on a regular basis, doing special things for them and showering them with attention.

She could picture the scene, and she played it over and over again in her mind. She'd answer the door, and there would be her husband with the same goofy grin her dad had displayed. Behind his back he'd have flowers or chocolates or maybe a new CD. She couldn't wait for that kind of life to begin.

But after five years, nothing remotely like that had happened in her marriage. Life had cheated her. Maybe it was time to start over.

Can you see why so many relationships crash at this point?

What Do You Want? Say It Out Loud

We're on dessert and still talking about these things. Both Brent and Carrie can address the issues and speak candidly to each other without getting angry or defensive. These matters are well in the past even though they still have a surprisingly high level of emotional power.

During our dinner, Brent consistently faults himself for the things he did wrong. "I took advantage of her, I really did," he says now, looking back at his irresponsible patterns as a young husband. "And as far as the kids go, I didn't have much interest in the crying, the night feedings, and the dirty diapers. I kept waiting for them to get old enough to play baseball."

By his own admission, Brent was immature and irresponsible. Yet his behavior and conduct was typical.

Does this surprise you? As it turns out, men aren't exactly hard-wired to hug and hold crying babies, to wake up at night and address problems, or to dive into their fair share of dirty diapers. It's a rare man who manages any one of these aspects, let alone two or three. Meanwhile, women—who certainly don't enjoy these things either!—tend to sacrifice their own needs and to nurture their children.

If I were advising a young wife about what to expect in her first years of marriage, this is the pattern I would try to prepare her for. And though a husband could certainly be more sensitive to his wife's needs and aggressive in meeting them, let's focus for a bit on what a wife can do to improve the situation.

"I was judging him in my head all that time, finding him guilty," Carrie admits as we sip our second or third refills of coffee. "I kept comparing him to my dad and to movies I'd seen. He didn't measure up, but I wasn't talking with him about my feelings. I wasn't telling him what I expected and needed.

"Let's face it; he didn't stand a chance. I didn't give him the opportunity to succeed. I just kept silently judging him, getting more and more depressed and frustrated and angry. There were so many things I wanted him to be, ways I wanted him to behave, and things I thought he would just automatically think of. But instead of telling him any of that, I resented him for being so thoughtless.

"Looking back, I'm not nearly as angry with him as I am disappointed in myself and my own choices. What was I thinking? I knew even then that I shouldn't expect him to read my mind. Yet somehow I expected him to understand what I needed and wanted and then to be proactive and creative and romantic all at the same time.

"I expected him to be superman, but I never even bothered to tell him how superman would behave if he did show up. I think that's my own fault, don't you?" Carrie asks rhetorically.

Expectations that go unspoken are likely to go unmet. Relational hopes and dreams that are never revealed aren't likely to be realized. Rather than picking up on their wives' feelings, men are likely to take the evidence as they find it. Are we having pretty good sex? Check. Am I making a decent salary and supporting my family? Check. Am I a pretty good husband by normal standards? Check. Am I staying faithful to her? Check.

So what else is there, anyway?

With the basics covered, husbands don't go looking for self-help books to figure out how they might improve. Instead, they refer to their own internal scorecards, formed by their own backgrounds and experiences and comparisons, and then rate their performance on the basis of their own judgments.

On his own internal husband-meter, a guy who can answer the above questions with a yes probably feels like he's succeeding. The questions may vary a bit from male to male, but in general, the idea seems to be to cover the big categories and not mess up in any spectacular ways.

"It's not like I'm cheating on her!" a husband will often tell us when his wife drags him into the marriage counseling office. He feels as if we should be congratulating him, not interrogating or accusing him. His wife may be starved for attention, affection, friendship, and intimacy, but according to the husband's internal husband-meter, he's doing okay.

Most husbands have a husband-meter. The man you married probably does, and he probably evaluates his marriage performance on the basis of the big issues in the list above. As long as he has a decent score on his scorecard, he's quite surprised when problems or issues arise.

"I thought we had a pretty good marriage," Brent says as he remembers how he felt just before his marriage almost collapsed. He's being honest and truthful about that. He is reporting just exactly how he felt and what he believed. According to his husband-meter, things were somewhere between "pretty good" and "above average."

For almost all guys, that's a passing grade. And for them, a passing grade is good enough—which is why wives need to talk with their husbands about their expectations. They need to be honest about what they're feeling, and they need to be specific about the ways they hope their husbands will think and behave.

Conversations like these are absolutely essential in any marriage, especially in the early years. The patterns you set at the beginning of your marriage may be with you for a very long time, so it's enormously helpful to establish positive patterns and helpful behaviors early on.

Wives need to talk about what they expect, explain how they feel, and spell out in clear detail what they're looking for. Even if a husband doesn't immediately rush to make these changes, at least he'll know what the scorecard looks like and how to put points on it. And all guys like to score. You already know this, right?

Without this kind of clear and specific guidance from you,

expecting your husband to read your mind, guess at your hopes, and begin to fulfill your childhood dreams is foolish. How would he possibly know these things? Have you told him what you're hoping for? Have you told him what you're expecting? Are you doing your part to help him succeed?

Begin at the Beginning If Possible

We explain to our server that we probably won't be leaving anytime soon. She brings us another round of decaf. Meanwhile, we're listening as Carrie continues to explore her version of what she might have done differently in the early days of her marriage.

"What if we had talked about these things during our premarital counseling?" she asks as we sip our coffee. "What if Brent stood at the altar already knowing the things I expected him to do as a husband and the ways I expected him to be as a father? But we didn't talk about any of these things. We met two times with the minister who was going to marry us. He told us that marriage was important, that divorce was out of the question, and that we ought to stay together for life. He kept asking us if we were serious and if we planned to take our marriage seriously.

"Like every other couple who wants to get married, we just told him yes. We weren't lying to him—of course we took marriage seriously. It's just that neither one of us really knew what to expect. And although I had some definite ideas about how Brent ought to treat me and care about me, I didn't bother to share those ideas with him. And during our two quick sessions of premarital counseling, our minister didn't ask me to share those things either."

Brent interjects at this point. "I'm not making excuses," he assures us. "I was just basically clueless. I really thought I was doing okay and our marriage was fine. No one told me how to judge my own behavior or how to evaluate my helpfulness or selfishness as a husband and then as a dad. Once I understood those things—and she had to tell me more than once before I began to understand how deep this was with her, and how serious it was to her, and how much it meant—once I understood those things, I started getting better at giving Carrie more of my attention. I wasn't good at it at first, but I did start working on it right away. And I think most guys, if they love their wives even a little bit, would do the same thing."

We wait to see if Carrie agrees. Not surprisingly, she does.

"He did change," she tells us. "His attitude changed almost immediately. He got all quiet when we talked about stuff, and I could almost see the wheels turning inside his mind. He was thinking about all of this, considering it, learning it. And almost immediately I started to notice little changes in the way he acted and treated me. We already had kids by this point, and I also saw him start deliberately spending more time with the boys. He also started offering to help me with some of the household chores, and I hadn't even talked about that!"

"Yeah," Brent admits, "I finally realized I had really messed up. So I was trying to earn some respect from her and trying to show her I could be different. I was making stuff up to see what would get the most response from her."

As you listen to that husband's description, can you almost see him recalibrating his internal husband-meter? He's changing the categories, figuring out how bad his score is, and calculating how to put more points on the scorecard.

Before, he didn't realize he was losing. Now he literally can't wait to start winning.

Guys like to succeed, to score, to win.

Finding Your Voice

Carrie returns to her narrative. "Here's what I wish I had done. Once we started seriously dating, I wish I had told him exactly what kinds of stuff my dad always did for my mom and why I liked that. I wish I had described my dad's behaviors and attitudes, his gifts and his surprises, his silly grins and his unexpected kindness. Once we were seriously talking about getting married, I wish I had told Brent how I thought the husband's role should play out. I had definite ideas about all this stuff from books, from movies, from my parents, and from my own opinions. I even took a marriage and family class in high school where we had to simulate a marriage, carry a baby around, go shopping for food and clothes, make a budget, and things like that.

"Based on my idyllic experiences, I already had a clear idea of how I wanted my husband to behave toward me. I knew how I wanted him to treat me, how I wanted him to lead our home and raise his children…everything. All of these expectations were just kind of stuffed up inside my head, but I never sat down and shared them with Brent—not before we got married and not even when my dreams started falling apart.

"Brent says he was clueless, but I think I'm really the one who meets that description," Carrie insists. "I can't believe how naive I was, how big a fool I was to think that any guy could just read my mind, figure out what I wanted, and start making it happen.

"How crazy is that? How unrealistic is that? But that's exactly what I was thinking and feeling. I was blaming my husband for not doing all these things even though I'd never told him what I wanted. Looking back, I feel like a total idiot."

"So if somebody makes a movie about our early days, maybe it will be called *Clueless in California* or something like that," Brent says, laughing. "But if that happens, I'll lobby for a sequel called *Making It Better in Missouri*. It would be completely different from the first movie."

Carrie laughs too. "Yeah, we got a bit smarter by the time we left California. I'm not saying we were a perfect couple or anything, but we sure were fighting a lot less. And I wasn't getting so depressed all the time."

Brent retakes the narrative. "Once we started talking about things and I realized what she was expecting of me and what she was hoping for, I started stepping up to the plate and making it happen. I'm not such a bad guy, really. I'm just a little slow on the uptake. I didn't have any sisters, I wasn't that close to my mom, and I had no idea how women thought. I still don't!

"But I often know what Carrie is thinking now because we talk about things, and she gives me a lot of information and a lot of feedback. She's pretty good at telling me when I mess up, and I'm helping her get better at telling me when I succeed. At least for me—and I think it's true for a lot of guys—I do a lot better when I feel like I'm succeeding. That motivates me to keep on trying, to keep on working, to keep getting better.

"At first, Carrie wasn't too good at handing out compliments, but she's gotten a lot better," Brent says, shooting his wife an impish grin.

"He's getting more compliments because he deserves them now," she insists, dishing it right back at him. "I'm telling him how well he does because it's often true!"

"Get a room!" David interjects loudly.

All four of us laugh, and we agree that the evening has been well spent.

Reflections for Your Personal Journey

1. Did you have any premarital counseling? If you did, what do you remember about it? Did the counselor or minister help you share your expectations with each other? How? Did he or she help you tell each other, clearly and explicitly, exactly how you thought a husband and wife would think and feel and act?

2. When you and your husband first began to talk seriously about being married someday, did you give him simple and clear explanations of the good ways you'd seen your own father fulfill his roles as a husband, a parent, and a man? Did you explain the way you thought husbands ought to behave toward their wives and their kids? Or did you take all this for granted, expecting your man to intuitively know how to behave once he became a husband and father?

3. During the first few months and years of your marriage, how often did you sit down and explain to your husband—not during a fight but when things were calm and reasonable— what you expected of him around the house, with the children, or in terms of gifts, holidays, and special events? How often did you give your husband the clues he needed in order to know how to put some points on his scorecard? How often did you give him the information he needed to be a success?

4. As you listened in on our dinner conversation in this chapter, did you identify with Brent and Carrie? Did any of their experiences together remind you of your own life and history? Have you made some of the same mistakes Carrie made? Are you still making those mistakes, or are you on the road to recovery?

5. Might your husband need specific clues and guidance from you right now about how to be a parent, how to be more

romantic, or how much time you would like for him to spend with just you? Are you expecting him to know these things even though you have never been clear, simple, and specific about them? (Don't count the things you told him while you were angry or while fighting with him. No one listens well or learns their best under these kinds of conditions. During an argument or a fight, most of us are too busy getting our feelings hurt and being defensive, so we don't learn well. Fights are not usually the best teaching moments in marriage.)

6. If you could give your husband two or three specific clues right now about how to reach or meet your expectations, what would they be? Grab a piece of paper and make a quick list of a few specific things you should tell your husband while you can still get his attention and make positive changes. Quit keeping things in your head and start putting things down on paper. Once they're on paper, find calm, peaceful times to talk about them with your man.

7. Have you discovered the power of giving your husband positive feedback? Most guys are a lot more motivated by praise than by nagging, criticism, or complaints. Spelling out clearly and specifically what your expectations are is okay. In fact, please do. But once you've done that, be sure to notice the changes your husband makes and compliment him for them. Don't wait for the big changes that anyone could see from a distance. Try to catch him making small positive changes and surprise him with a genuine compliment and a soft word of thanks. When a guy succeeds, he is motivated to keep on trying.

What You Don't See in Yourself: Unconscious Pride

We first meet Maria when she invites us to her home, asking for our advice and counsel regarding her marriage of nearly a dozen years. A friend at her local church referred her to us.

When we first speak with Maria on the phone, we raise the obvious question: "Will your husband be with us as we meet?"

"Oh, no," she replies, "he's not willing to get any kind of help. He keeps telling me that he's not the one with the problem!"

After conversation and prayer, we set a time and a date to meet with Maria. A few days later, we drive north along the I-15, praying for a woman we've never met and a marriage that we've been told is in deep trouble. Beside us the rock-strewn mountains of Southern California are green with bright, fresh foliage. It's been an abnormally rainy winter, ending three years of drought.

We pull off the freeway at Carmel Mountain Ranch, a planned development of beautiful shops and attractive restaurants. We merge into the busy afternoon traffic flow as we make our way north along a wide, tree-lined parkway. This upscale neighborhood in Rancho Bernardo is bursting with the fragrant blooms of a lush California spring: flowers, vines, trees, and grass. David and I comment on the metaphor of new birth, praying this theme together as we drive toward the home of a new friend we are about to meet for the first time. If God can bring so much beautiful new life to the desert hills of northern San Diego, causing the parched trees to flourish with colorful blossoms, surely He can accomplish the same kind of miracle amid the dry places of a 12-year marriage relationship that's gone stale.

As the shops and restaurants give way to homes and condos, we catch the scent of fresh lilac in bloom. We switch off the air conditioning in our car, roll down the windows, and drive a bit more slowly to savor the aroma.

Maria's home is at the end of a quiet cul-de-sac that we reach from a narrow street in a gated community. As we enter the code Maria gave us, the wrought-iron gate swings open. When we pull into Maria's driveway, we are a bit overwhelmed by the 180-degree views. To the north and east, rock-strewn mountains tower over us, covered in a fresh carpet of green and bathed in the rays of early afternoon sunshine. Spreading out between us and the mountains is a verdant valley of well-manicured homes curled along tree-lined streets. The scene is peaceful and Mediterranean. It's like Tuscany but with nicer, newer houses. Palms and pines sprout up along the horizon for as far as the eye can see.

Descending into the contours of the valley, the tees and fairways of a freshly mown golf course wind their way down a gentle decline. Very few golfers are playing this afternoon, so the course is eerily quiet. Both of us admire the view for a moment before David breaks the silence with a wry but accurate observation.

"I could write here," he muses, entranced by the scenic vistas on every side. I nod my head in agreeable consent.

We ring Maria's doorbell, halfway expecting a staff person to answer. But Maria herself greets us only a few seconds after our first ring. She's barefoot, wearing a flowing white dress, and at the moment she's cradling a steaming mug of coffee. We've only spoken to Maria on the phone, but she greets us as if we're already old friends.

"Please come in," Maria invites us, smiling broadly. "By the way, do you two drink coffee? I forgot to ask you."

"We'd love some coffee!" I inform our hostess, smiling at her. Behind us the solid oak door swings shut, and we find ourselves in a paneled entry hall with high ceilings and hanging tapestries. I catch the aroma of Maria's frothy drink.

"Why don't we have our little talk in the kitchen," Maria asks us politely, leading the way through her spacious home. We follow her past an alcove filled with beautiful art and then a study lined with custom-made bookshelves. Toward the end of a long hallway, we enter a dream kitchen that is larger than many homes, its floors lined with large travertine tiles set in a diagonal pattern.

"We could just take our coffee at the counter if you'd like," Maria suggests, showing us to a half-dozen bar stools grouped along the curved corner of a granite countertop. While Maria steps away to fill our coffee mugs, David runs his fingers along the edges of the granite, admiring the stonecutter's work. Maria's kitchen countertops are a beautiful shade of brown, lighter than David's coffee but darker than mine, streaked with bits of black and tan and ivory and gray. The stone's surfaces are highly polished, but the edges have been left rough-hewn and natural.

"What color do they call this?" I ask Maria, pointing to the granite counters.

Maria smiles brightly. "The supplier called it cola when we were deciding which to use," she remembers. "I think they got the name right, don't you? It always reminds me of the foam on top of an icy cold cola!"

David and I admire the stone as Maria busies herself pouring our drinks.

"Do you take any sweetener?" Maria asks. "All we have is some Stevia," she adds apologetically. "It's the only kind of sugar my husband will let me buy."

David glances at me discreetly. So much for the pleasantries, his glance seems to imply. It looks like our counseling session will begin sooner rather than later. After all, we've come here to work, not to sip caffeine.

Drawing in the Dirt

Maria gathers her dress around her while she seemingly also gathers her thoughts. David takes a long sip of coffee and stares out the kitchen window at a group of calla lilies blooming along the edges of the pavers in the courtyard. He seems fully present in the moment and yet lost in a private thought. When a counselee is slow to open up, my husband is reliably calm and patient. I always picture Jesus, bending down to write in the dirt as the adulteress is dragged before Him by her accusers. It's a scene that interests me as a woman and as a counselor.

Christ loves this woman, but He is unwilling to intrude or to invade her privacy. Scripture tells us that she was "caught in the very act" of committing adultery, so she might not be dressed decently. By averting His gaze from her sudden embarrassment and shame, Jesus is protecting this woman's privacy. I've always admired Jesus's response in that moment, utterly unplanned and yet so composed, so gracious, so merciful.

David waits patiently for Maria to be ready to speak.

The three of us sit together in silence for a few moments, long enough to hear a distant clock chime the quarter-hour with resounding clarity.

"I'm not really sure where I should begin," Maria says hesitantly, suddenly seeming to hold back tears. Without thinking, I reach out to take her hand. Maria welcomes my hand in hers, squeezing mine tightly. She struggles to keep her composure.

Both of us wait; no words are forming.

"Why don't we start with prayer?" David suggests, and the three of us bow our heads. After a moment's pause, David begins to pray aloud. He asks that God's light will invade our space, showing us clearly how to proceed. David requests that God's wisdom will illuminate us, showing us wisely how to act and speak in this moment and in the balance of the time we will share this day. His voice is calm, and his words are clear. He is talking to God as though our Father were sitting with us on one of the tall bar stools in Maria's comfortable and expansive kitchen.

I am not aware of whether the prayer is long or short, yet the room feels different now. Does the temperature actually increase? When God's children seek Him in prayer, the whole environment often seems to be bathed in His holy presence. The three of us enter such a moment together, and we can suddenly tell God is in the house. His Spirit joins with us as we seek His wisdom, His guidance, His will.

Strangers in the Same House

Maria begins her story as we conclude our prayer time.

"Perry was so different when we first got married," Maria tells us. "He was much more romantic, much more patient with me, much more involved around the house. He laughed a lot, and he made me feel like I was the most important person on the whole planet. He made me feel like I was the *only* person on the whole planet…" She dabs at her eyes with a tissue, breaking her narrative for a moment. David's body language is open, listening, and attentive.

"That was a long time ago," Maria continues. "It's been a long time since he paid any attention to me at all or even noticed I'm alive. He used to come up behind me and kiss me or tell me how nice I looked," she tells us. "He used to compliment me all the time or bring me little gifts. But that hasn't happened in so long now…I can't remember the last time he just kissed me for no reason, the last time he just came up beside me in the kitchen or the family room and just wrapped his arms around me and told me he loved me.

"It's like he's abandoned me completely," Maria realizes. "Like he's left me but without moving out of our home. At the end of the day he comes back here, but it's like he never really arrives. He is so cold, so impersonal, so businesslike now in everything he says to me. It's all about our schedules or who's taking the kids to what practice or what game. It's always about getting out our calendars and marking down the dates and times of our children's events."

Maria pauses for a long moment.

"I just feel abandoned," she continues. "That's exactly the word I'm trying to find. I feel totally and completely abandoned, like I'm a single mom raising these kids on my own. There's no one at my side, no one to help me make the big choices or even the simple everyday decisions about the house or the kids. I have to do all these things by myself. If you followed us around all day on a typical day, you'd realize that I'm the one raising these kids. I'm the one running this house. I'm the one doing everything it takes to have a marriage and raise a family. There's no one else helping out—it's just me!" She pauses as her declaration echoes through an empty home.

"I'm so lonely," Maria confesses. "It's like I thought I married my best friend, but then my friend completely disappeared. In his place there is the businessman who makes deals, talks on the phone, and is gone from our lives a lot. I look around at this beautiful place and realize how blessed I am. My husband earns a lot of money in his business. He has a gift for making money. He always has.

"But why is it always me?" she asks rhetorically. "When anything happens around here, or anyone cares about the kids, or anyone makes a plan that helps the family or gets something done—I'm the one who does all that.

"I am a single mother with a wedding ring on my finger," Maria suddenly says, as if saying it for the first time. "I'm a single mom who just happens to have a husband living under the same roof.

"It's never been about the money with me," she continues without waiting for our response. "I could give all of this up, this huge house, everything else too, if he would just hold my hand sometimes, or talk softly to me at night, or hug me for no reason. I wouldn't even need the sex—and it's been a long time since there was any of *that* around this house—I wouldn't even need the sex if he would just hold me and hug me and talk to me, if he would just be here for me."

Maria's voice trails off, and she is lost again in silence. Instinctively,

I reach out again to touch her arm. Maria, without looking at me, takes my hand in hers and just squeezes it. I realize that she's lacking and missing a simple human touch—the ordinary everyday affection that helps us know we are loved. I am praying for her while David and I wait for her next words.

From Party to Pity

Somewhere far off in the house, the same distant clock chimes again. I have not been keeping track of the time, and more time has passed than I realized. David has a stunningly accurate clock in his head. He usually knows the time without glancing at his watch, but at this moment, he too seems unaware of time.

Maria sniffs loudly and gets control of her emotions.

"Here's how it really is," she says, almost as an afterthought. "I'm the only one who does any of the work around here. I'm the only one who cares whether we have a good marriage—or whether we even stay married to each other at all!

"I'm the only one who cooks and cleans and drives the kids to their practices and games. I'm the only one who shops and chooses and decides what we need. I thought marriage was supposed to be a partnership, but it's like I don't have a partner anymore. I just have me. That's not why I got married—to be alone. I got married to have someone around that I could talk to, someone who would listen to me, someone who would care about me and care for me. Is that asking too much?"

Maria is quiet again for a moment, and then changes her tone completely.

"Sometimes I think I could have an affair or something, right here under his nose, and he wouldn't even notice it was happening. His whole life now is so separate, so distant, so removed from me—it's almost like we're two completely different people, two strangers living together in this one great big house. We're not really together anymore, not in any way that matters. I could have some new lover here all day, and Perry would never even find out it was happening,"

Maria says with disgust. "It's not like he cares about what I'm doing all day or where I go when he's not around."

Suddenly I'm not happy with where this conversation is going. When a woman brings up the idea of having an affair, even as a possibility, I tend to get nervous. How is a person supposed to respond to that? Judgment isn't helpful, but agreement is out of the question also. I know this woman is just thinking out loud, but it doesn't sit well with me. I'm praying that God gives us wisdom in this moment.

David suddenly interjects a surprising question. "Do you keep your wedding pictures nearby?" he asks our hostess.

Maria brightens immediately, nodding her head as she smiles.

"Yes," she says. "I get them out sometimes, just to look at them and remember happier days."

"Could we look at those pictures?" David suggests. "Just briefly?"

Maria agrees, easing out of the bar stool and striding purposely toward another room of the house. I watch her disappear, realizing once again just how large this home is. I'm guessing it is 5000 or 6000 square feet, maybe more, and all or most of it is on one level. The house sprawls out around us in all directions with sunny corridors leading to partially seen rooms and oversized furnishings.

David lowers his voice to a whisper. "We won't look at these pictures for very long," he suggests to me in a conspiratorial tone. "But I think a few minutes of time with her wedding photos just might be good therapy for her right now."

Maria rejoins us quickly, carrying two leather-bound photo albums with gilt edges and brass bindings. The albums themselves have an Old World sense about them, reflecting the craftsmanship and excellence from another era. Beautifully made and heavy, they're the nicest albums I've seen. I can't help wondering what she paid for them. Does Walmart sell albums like these? I don't think so.

"We don't need to look at everything right now. Just show us a few of your favorite pictures," David recommends. "Let's take a moment and get to know the two of you on your wedding day. Can you remember what you were thinking and feeling in that moment?"

"Oh yes," Maria assures us, as she begins a spirited recounting of her courtship and wedding to the dashing groom we see in the photos. Her entire manner is different. She laughs occasionally as she points out relatives and friends from her wedding party.

"You should see that one today," Maria says with a laugh, pointing to an attractive young woman in a picture of the bridesmaids. "She's put on at least fifty pounds! She had a bunch of kids and just let herself go. She doesn't look anything like that anymore!"

Charting the Changes: Maria's List

Fifteen minutes later, David gently returns us to our primary purpose.

"So, obviously," David says quietly as we finish looking at a particular photo of the bride and groom and their godparents, "a lot has changed in your relationship since you first got married. What's different now? How would you describe the primary changes in your marriage from that day until right now?"

Maria, calmer and much more composed after this brief interlude of looking at pictures and talking about her wedding, immediately begins her description of the many changes she's observed in the couple's life together. After listening patiently for what seems like a long time but is probably only about ten minutes, David asks her to stop and categorize things for a moment.

"So can you list what you would say are the top three changes since then, the three most important or most significant changes you've observed in your marriage relationship?"

Maria pauses, and I sense her beginning to sort and sift these things in her spirit. She's a verbal processor, so for a while we just listen as she talks about a wide range of issues, describing ways her husband has evolved and changed since the early days of the marriage. For this section of our time together, I carry most of the conversational load. After Maria and I talk for a while, she lists the three major changes that she can observe from the start of the union until today.

1. I'm the only one who cares about our relationship. I'm the only one who ever tries to be intimate or friendly or even nice.

2. I'm the only one who plans the schedules for the kids, takes them to all their appointments, listens to their dentists and their coaches, and cheers for their soccer games and their dance recitals. It's like they don't have two parents, just one. I'm the only parent they've got.

3. I'm the only one who does any work around the house. When Perry comes home, he doesn't lift a finger. I'm the one who cleans up after him. I'm the one who cleans up after the kids. I'm the one who plans the meals and fixes the little things that need repair. If anything needs doing around this place, I'm the one who actually does it. Just me.

Maria pauses after finishing this short list, seemingly worn out just from considering the sorry state of her marriage relationship. She lets out a long sigh of self-pity or frustration or both, I cannot tell which. She slumps back in her chair and seemingly has nothing more to say for a while.

Patiently, David says nothing at first. If you asked him about this, he would tell you that he's waiting for a teachable moment. Such moments are rare in counseling, but they do exist. They are definitely worth waiting for.

After more than two decades of counseling and learning together with my husband, I often know where David is going in the flow of a conversation with a new client. This is one of those moments, and I can't wait to watch him turn the corner and address the main concern here. I know he'll do it gently. I marvel at David's ability to empathize with someone yet also to gently uncover and explore unhelpful patterns and habits.

"Maria," David says after a long pause of his own, "Lisa and I didn't drive over here today to yell at you; we came here to listen to you. We want to be as helpful to you as we can." David is choosing his words very carefully. His attitude is friendly, open, relaxed, caring. He is maintaining eye contact with Maria and clearly demonstrating empathy, compassion, and understanding. He actually is a grandfather, and today he definitely comes across as one.

"Anyway," David continues, "I want to ask you a very important question right now. And that's all it is, by the way—it's a question. I hope you'll think about it and then give us the best answer you can think of."

Maria nods her head, agreeing to this.

"Maria," David prompts her gently, "I notice that you listed three items that you are doing pretty well around here and that your husband is doing poorly. All three of them follow that format: Here's what I'm doing right, and here's what my husband is doing wrong. The pattern is very clear. Did you notice that as you talked to us?"

David says this in a relaxed, conversational, and friendly tone. He doesn't have an attitude of reproof or correction. He sounds as if he's commenting on a butterfly dabbing at a nearby flower or a hummingbird fluttering outside the window. He's making a simple observation and not an accusation. I marvel at how often he can keep people from feeling defensive while he explains their core issues. He pauses, unhurried and genial.

"So I guess my question is this," David explains to our hostess. "Would you say that your behavior toward your husband today is pretty much exactly the way it was in the early days of your marriage? Are you as loving to him, as kind to him, and as joyous and positive with him as you were in those first few weeks and months of your life together? When you interact with your husband, either in front of the kids or behind closed doors, do you look and sound toward him pretty much the same way you looked and sounded when you first got together?"

The room is absolutely still; the precise quietness is tangible.

"Now that you've listed some of the big problems that bother you about your husband's behavior and patterns," David says in his quietest and kindest voice, "I guess what I'm asking you today is this: How have *you* been behaving lately in your part of this marriage? How do *you* speak and act when you're dealing with your husband at home? If we followed you around with a video camera and recorded you as you talked with Perry, what would we see and hear?"

David completes the question, still as calm and unruffled as a morning pond. Gently, the bomb is dropped, and now we wait for the aftershocks. My husband the counselor is supernaturally relaxed. I breathe a silent prayer for all of us. The next few moments will tell us whether anything useful is happening.

Aftershocks: Living on the Fault Lines

In the moments that follow, Maria will experience the beginning of a paradigm shift. She will start to see the world around her in an entirely new way. Her situation and her circumstances probably won't change right away, but Maria's view of those circumstances will become entirely different. When counseling works, when it is successful and fruitful, it leads toward moments like this—moments when you look at the same reality but see it in a whole new way.

For a surprised Maria, the paradigm shift begins almost immediately. She lets out a long sigh and eases herself gently out of a nearby bar stool. "Um…" is as much as she says at first. Clearly this entire line of thought has caught her off guard. She called us because she wanted to talk about her husband and his abandonment of her, his emotional and sexual distance from her, and all the ways she had become the primary caregiver and provider in the family.

Now, with little warning, an entirely different set of questions is suddenly in play. Is Maria herself the same carefree and positive person she was in the early days of her marriage? Does she approach her husband with respect and appreciation or with disappointment, contempt, or pride? Maria takes a few steps across the kitchen floor and then a few steps back. Even her stride reveals that she is uncertain, searching, questioning.

Like many other frustrated wives, Maria probably has high hopes that a counselor will issue some official orders to her husband. She's hoping for some binding and useful instructions for him, such as "Go home and make love to your wife tonight! Start paying attention to her needs, man! Quit being so busy at work and come home to your kids! Take better care of your family!"

Instead, my gentle husband has raised a thought-provoking and unexpected question in this quiet kitchen today. "What about your own behavior?" David has asked Maria. "Are you still treating your husband exactly the same way you did in the early days of your marriage relationship? Are you kind and gentle and caring toward him?"

Clearly, this is a line of questioning that Maria has not even considered until now. She sips the remains of her coffee as she paces the kitchen floor first one way and then off in the other direction. She remains within easy earshot of us, but she hasn't formed a reply yet. She is pacing, staring, thinking, realizing.

Her behavior? Why is this even an issue? After all, she's not the one who's being distant. She's not the one who stays away from the house all day. She's not the one who seems so impersonal and cold, so reserved and shut away. She's not the one who is absent from the normal everyday duties of raising the children and running the household. So why are we talking about her behavior? She's the one who's out there doing everything right! She's the one who ought to win an award or something!

We can almost watch it happen as these ideas and questions form in Maria's mind, yet she appears to be considering the question with unusual care and surprising openness. Light dawns in her heart, and David and I are present to witness the moment when Maria's horizon expands toward new hope.

"I haven't been nice to him in a long time," Maria tells us eventually. Her voice is so quiet I can hardly hear her. I have trouble discerning what she's said. "I haven't been nice to him at all."

Maria stares down at the floor. Once again, I sense that tears are about to begin flowing. This time, for whatever reason, I feel prompted to *not* invade her privacy, *not* reach out to grab her hand.

This is Maria's moment, a season of personal discovery and private revelation.

Maria gulps and keeps her gaze focused steadily at the floor.

"I have never realized any of this until right this minute," she says, struggling to find her voice. "I've been so focused on all the ways he was disappointing me and disappointing the kids, I haven't even noticed the way I've been treating him. I never thought about this at all until right now," she asserts.

We wait; neither David nor I interrupt Maria's monologue.

"Oh, my God..." she says with a low groan. "Oh, my God..." It's all the prayer she can utter at the moment.

Like the bright rays of afternoon sunlight invading Maria's kitchen, God's illumination arrives to clearly reveal the condition of her relationship. Maria is having an "aha moment" while safely in the company of two people who genuinely care about her and who are not judging her or feeling superior to her.

"The ground is level at the foot of the cross," is one of my husband's favorite sayings, and he lives the truth of that in the way he relates to people. My husband, perhaps more than anyone I've ever known, treats everyone with equal compassion, regardless of their economic status, level of education, family history, or any other trait. He is warm and nice with the few wealthy people we know, yet he shows genuine respect especially for "the least of these" and those who are down-and-out. He treats even the guilty people we meet as though he himself were the guilty one.

Maria is silent for a long while.

"Well," David says after allowing for a sufficient pause. "Maybe we're making some progress here. Maybe we've found what we should work on together as we begin to think about your marriage relationship."

Moving Forward: The Healing Power of Time

That first appointment was some time ago, and since then, Maria has radically changed the way she thinks and feels about her husband

and the way she describes him to others. These days, when Maria points out a fault in her marriage or a problem in the relationship, she identifies an area in which she can improve or she needs to get a clue. This has become a hallmark of our times with Maria. Although she no longer seeks regular counseling with us, we interact with her frequently, so we're aware of the condition of her marriage.

By God's grace, the health of her marriage is changing for the better on a daily basis. It is much different than it was on the day we met.

For Maria, the primary confronting realization was that unconscious pride had somehow become a part of her life. Maria went through all the motions of her day, interacting with her children and mother and friends while believing Perry was failing. Meanwhile, she pictured herself as the heroine of the family.

In Maria's own description of her daily reality, she told us she was the one who cared, who worked on the relationship, and who was raising the kids. Maria made positive statements about herself in each of these areas.

"Look what I'm achieving," Maria was saying without realizing it. "Look how noble and positive and good I'm being. I'm doing all the right things!" Meanwhile, Maria was pointing to Perry's deficiencies and inappropriate behavior. "Look who's not helping me around here. Look who isn't doing his part in this relationship. Look who doesn't measure up to what any normal woman would expect from her husband."

Maria was unconsciously pointing with pride to her own behavior in her marriage and family. She was also unconsciously pointing a finger of accusation at Perry. "He's not carrying his load around here. I'm the one who's being responsible!"

Can you see the problem with Maria's perspective? Can you understand the danger of her distorted view of her world? In Maria's inner narrative, she was the heroine, and Perry was the villain. Even if justice never arrived in this lifetime, everyone would know that Maria was the good guy and Perry was obviously the bad guy. Didn't you hear all the proof? Surely Maria deserves our admiration.

The Deadliest Sins Are Hidden

Unconscious pride is one of the deadliest sins in marriage and in daily life. Our pride may be painfully obvious to everyone around us, but we ourselves are often the last to discover it. Meanwhile, we aren't the only ones it hurts. Our unconscious pride also hurts others, especially those we truly care about.

This is why we must confront our pride before we do anything else, why we must apply the lesson of the log and speck to our own lives. After all, are we perfect wives as we go about our daily lives? Really, have you ever met a perfect wife?

I'm not talking about appearances, about always being perfectly dressed or about having supermodel good looks, dazzling teeth, and great hair. The question is not whether you've seen the visual image of a perfect wife, but rather whether you've ever met a woman who actually measures up to that ideal. Of course, no one does. We all have areas to grow in.

Maybe, like the rest of us, you've been operating with unconscious pride in your life. If so, it's time to look in the mirror with humility and new understanding, confessing your guilt and making plans to see things much differently.

Ready to look in the mirror? Here's an application section with helpful questions for you to explore.

Reflections for Your Personal Journey

1. As you read through Maria's story, did anything she said sound like anything you might say? Do you ever talk about your life the way Maria talked about hers? How do you describe your life to others?

2. When you talk to your children about your family life, do you point to the things you're doing right and not the things you want to improve? Do you mention the things your husband is doing wrong and not the things he's doing well?

3. When you're with your mom or your closest friends, do you tend to present yourself as the one who is trying in the relationship, the one who is doing all the work around the house? When you're describing your marriage to your friends, are you usually the hero?

4. How long have you thought your behavior in your marriage was mostly right and your husband's behavior was mostly wrong? How did you reach these conclusions? Even if your observations are accurate, can you see any unconscious pride in your heart?

5. Have you taken a good long look at the way you behave in your marriage? Have you asked God to review the way you talk to your husband, the way you think and feel about him? Are you ready to have God show you any pockets of pride in your own heart?

6. Do you see yourself as a better marriage partner than your husband is? Does he behave worse than you do? If so, what does this attitude say about the possibility of unconscious pride deep within you?

7. Perhaps you've never noticed a prideful spirit in your tone or actions. Think of one or two of your closest friends or family members who might be open enough to give you an honest assessment and help you move forward.

The Power to Destroy:
Unrelenting Criticism

We're scheduled to teach at a Friday evening marriage enrichment event in the Phoenix metro area and then to preach at the weekend services for a large suburban congregation. The pastor has asked us to talk about family relationships during the worship services, and David is looking forward to doing so. An ordained minister, David has performed almost 400 weddings worldwide. I love hearing him preach, and though the weekend will be busy for both of us, we are looking forward to it.

We've taught and preached at this church often and have made many friends there, so we look forward to visiting them during our working trip to Arizona. As our well-traveled Honda minivan winds through the rocky canyons and tight mountain passes of Interstate 8 in Southern California, David and I talk about and pray for several of the couples we hope to connect with during almost a week in the Valley of the Sun. When our weekend work is done, we're staying over for a few days of rest and renewal in the desert. We'll have time to socialize with anyone who wants to have coffee or a meal with us.

We pray for and text one of the couples we've met on our previous journeys. I look up just as we pass a hillside wind farm near Campo, California. The turbines are revolving steadily at a brisk pace, generating much-needed power for a growing section of the country. Almost immediately after sending the text, I hear the buzz of an incoming message. Who replies so quickly?

"When can U come 4 dinner?"

Half a dozen text messages later, we have a dinner date in Arizona after our working weekend concludes—a time to reconnect and celebrate. Even better from David's perspective, the couple is inviting us to dinner at their home on the night of a Celtics game during the NBA playoffs. If you've heard David speak in any venue, you probably already know that my husband is a hard-core Celtics fan, cheering for the guys in green through good seasons and bad.

In our home, basketball is almost a religion, especially Boston Celtics basketball. Dinner with friends and a Celtics game…this is an invitation from heaven itself. After a busy weekend of serving and helping, we'll sit out on a well-appointed patio, watch a beautiful desert sunset, and then head indoors to witness yet another Celtics triumph during the playoffs. This will be a wonderful opportunity to recharge our emotional and spiritual batteries and enjoy a nice dinner that is purely recreational.

Or so we believe.

Getting the Details Right

The marriage event goes well. The host church includes a wonderful meal with the Friday evening session and choses a high-end caterer who is also a member of the congregation. The result is a fresh and attractive presentation of first-class vegetables, salads, meats, and breads. The dessert bar, presented in four separate stations in the four corners of our event venue, equals anything you'd find at an upscale Hyatt or Hilton.

Our 90-minute presentation is punctuated with much laughter, frequent applause, and a standing ovation at the conclusion. "They were happy before I got up there," David says. "I think they were cheering for the food, but I'll take it as a good sign." It's our first time through a new series of PowerPoint slides for our Soul-Mate Marriage workshop, and both of us are happy with the flow, the graphics, the organization, and the outcome.

The weekend worship services also go well, although after preaching the same sermon four times in a row, David admits he's somewhat worn out. One of the things I value about the man I married is that even when he preaches the same sermon four times in one weekend, he manages to make it slightly different each time. If you attended all four of the services as I always do, you'd be treated to different jokes, different intros, and sometimes even different stories or illustrations, but all in the format of the same outline.

"I'm easily bored," David explains. "And if I'm preaching something that bores me, how can I expect the audience to be interested?"

The lead pastor of the Phoenix church is very happy with the weekend and its results, and he invites us to come back again soon. We always enjoy mixing with old friends, meeting some new ones, and taking in the scenic beauty of Phoenix and its suburbs. The nearby mountains, rocky cliffs, palm trees, and silhouettes of saguaro cactus plants are absolutely beautiful, especially during sunrise or sunset.

After a weekend featuring a very full schedule and a lot of intense work, both David and I are looking forward to the Tuesday night dinner and Celtics game with our friends. We don't know them well, but we've sensed a genuine connection in our past times with them. Getting ready for dinner at our Scottsdale hotel, both of us decide to dress casually. As we arrive, we can almost taste the delicious barbecue meal.

We're ready to relax, but unknown to us, this evening will be anything but relaxing.

Lifestyles of the Rich and Famous: Desert Edition

Our hosts for this evening live in Anthem, a planned subdivision on the north fringes of Phoenix, spread out along Interstate 17 as it heads toward Sedona and Flagstaff. Anthem has numerous water features, a large community park, and some of the best walking trails I've seen. In the middle of the desert, even on the warmest of days, the trails wind through lush green grass, sparkling water-falls, and cascading ponds that grow as they flow downhill. Wild-life is always abundant here. I usually see groups of rabbits in the tall grass and a variety of ducks in the various ponds. For children and their parents, one major benefit of the community park is a narrow-gauge train that winds slowly through the best parts of the scenery.

"I think I want to get up early and walk some of these trails tomor-row morning," I tell David as we turn off the freeway onto one of Anthem's wide, tree-lined parkways.

"Great idea," he agrees.

We decide to make a quick stop at Fry's Signature Market, one of our favorite grocery stores in North America. For us, the Fry's Signa-ture in Anthem is almost a destination in itself. The sprawling store sells furniture, sporting goods, books, and a variety of other items in addition to a fabulous selection of grocery items. At the coffee bar, you can lounge on comfy leather sofas and catch up with Oprah or the day's news on a large plasma television.

We're early, so David and I stroll around the store for a while, marveling at the wide, clean aisles leading to attractively priced gro-ceries. Although our friends have declined our offer to bring some-thing, we pick up some flowers and also a few choices of decaf diet colas and sparkling waters. Both of us have learned from our moth-ers never to greet our hosts empty-handed.

Leaving the parking lot at Fry's, we curl north on the Anthem parkway toward a prominent mountain. The late-afternoon sun slants through a nearby wash, and we see bright red blooms on some of the cactus plants. Like San Diego, Phoenix has had rain lately. The result here is a flowering desert featuring unusual and rarely seen vegeta-tion in a wide array of colors and shapes.

We marvel at the beauty all around us, realizing anew why thought-ful and intelligent people choose to live in this place despite the heat, which challenges even the hardiest souls during half the year. Anthem, Scottsdale, Chandler, and Queen Creek offer scenic vistas, inviting horizons, and year-round attractive communities.

At the entrance to a country-club community, I read the gate code from a text message, and David enters it on a keypad. The wrought-iron gate slides open along a narrow track just wide enough for one car to safely enter. We are scarcely into the community before the gate slides closed behind us.

We've interacted with our hosts several times here in Arizona, and they've stopped by our home when traveling through Southern California. So although we may not know them well, we've had several casual contacts with them in two different states, usually sharing a meal or coffee.

The homes grow increasingly larger with each new bend in the road. Lush vegetation springs up out of the desert, and a rocky waterfall adorns the junction of two main roads. The developers of this newer community fully understand how to please the eye and welcome the visitor.

Watching the desert vistas unfold in all directions, we feel welcome here. Knowing our evening would include much food, we've dined lightly all day. We're ready for barbecue and basketball. But we're not ready for what this evening will actually hold.

Thou Shalt Not Covet (If Possible)

We have barely turned off the ignition before Darlene is out of her house and rushing down the sidewalk to greet us at our car.

"I'm so glad you could come over while you're in town!" she gushes as she hugs me. "We've been so eager to show you our new place."

David and I gather up the drinks and flowers we've brought and follow our hostess along a curved sidewalk through an amazingly landscaped front yard. I comment on the lovely red blooms sprouting up from the cactus plants.

"Aren't they beautiful? We've lived in this area for eight years, and we've never seen it like this. This is the most rain we've ever had!"

Five minutes later we are touring a sprawling single-level home that occupies one of the largest lots in the country club. The twelfth and fourteenth greens of a championship-level golf course border this home, set off by see-through fences that clearly display the lush grass of the fairways. Our hosts are active golfers, and their choice of this home is deliberate.

"We weren't really looking for something this big," Darlene explains as we tour the fourth or fifth bedroom of her new home. "But once we saw this lot, with the golf course views from every room, we just couldn't help ourselves!"

The decline in real estate values hit hard in America's west, resulting in numerous foreclosures and short sales across California, Arizona, and Nevada. Darlene—we still haven't seen Jerry, her husband, yet this evening—explains that they purchased this home during a pre-short-sale period, agreeing with the lender on a reasonable sales price, so the home avoided the foreclosure process. When she casually tells us the final price for this sprawling and nearly new house, my husband audibly gasps.

"You've got to be kidding me," David stammers. "Please tell me it's not true."

The economic downturn has made Arizona real estate an attractive value for the fortunate few who can afford to jump in. Apparently, our friends here are among the privileged. They've upscaled their lifestyle considerably since our last visit, and their previous home was also large and new. Their prior home had more than enough space for the two of them. The new home, larger and nicer in every way, is decorated like the fine houses in the pages of *Architectural Digest*.

David is still shaking his head over the price. "This would cost two million or more almost anywhere in San Diego County," David says quietly, "even with the market still depressed."

"We've got the ocean," I remind my husband as he stares off into space.

My efforts to help my husband avoid coveting are completely doomed when we finally greet Jerry. Darlene has been leading us on a very thorough tour, even opening her closet doors to reveal wood or wire storage cubicles and clever design. I realize that when I show people through our home, I never open my closet doors. But maybe, I suppose, if David and I had showplace closets like these, with recessed lighting and crown molding and multilevel built-in shoe racks, I too would feature my closets when giving guests a tour of our home. Maybe.

Meanwhile, our tour has finally exhausted the enclosed area of this capacious home. We are outdoors now, walking along an infinity pool that burbles quietly into a small stream, constantly overflowing so that the stream is fed with fresh water as it curves through a xeriscaped backyard.

David is completely silent. I know he's found yet another spot where he'd love to write a book or article or essay. He is picturing himself seated by the pool as the sun rises over the nearby mountains. But he is about to be blown away yet again, destroying any hope of avoiding a moment or two of outright, commandment-busting coveting. Our tour ends—or David might say it actually begins—with the most amazing man-cave in the history of…well, mankind.

More like a Man Mansion

Jerry is beaming, ready to show us his private enclave. "Come right on in," he insists.

We're walking into what I first believed to be an oversized gazebo perched in the midst of the pool area. Clearly, I was mistaken. This would be the mother of all gazebos if it were one, with a ceiling height of perhaps 16 or 18 feet. Yet the inside is completely finished, with four different alcoves and a main area that features a sunken living room space with a central fire pit.

An indoor fire pit? The raised center roof of the gazebo-like structure has screened, open-air windows. Due to some tiny loophole in the local fire code, this structure is not considered to be part of the house and is actually classified somewhat like an outdoor tool shed or picnic area. As anyone can clearly see, this arrangement is nothing like that at all. But apparently within this particular space, building an indoor fire is legal.

Wow.

The central living area and one of the four alcoves have giant-screen televisions, each surrounded by plump leather recliners and sofas. The alcove is set up like a media room, with several rows of reclining leather chairs, each with a beverage holder. I find myself hoping that we'll be watching the basketball game in that space, although I'd much rather curl up in front of a chick flick in that setting.

The gazebo sprawls out in all directions. If I were watching a movie with my daughters or my girlfriends, David could be somewhere else in here, watching the Celtics or reading the newspaper. Several other parties could be happening here at the same time— there's plenty of room for all of us.

Meanwhile, our friendly host interrupts my daydreaming.

"I think we'll watch the game out here," Jerry insists, pointing to the central living area. "It's the biggest screen we have outdoors, although we do have a larger one in the den, back at the house." He is clearly giddy with delight at the chance to show us his man-cave.

"Hey, while you two look around, I need to stay closer to the grill because the meat is almost ready. We're having chicken kabobs tonight and a flaming dessert later. Is free-range chicken okay with everybody?"

It's a rhetorical question, but our answer is definitely yes.

Jerry leads us to an alcove that features a large dining table, heavy and ornate. Each chair is an armchair with extensive detailing on the arms and legs and backs. The fabric on the tufted cushions is exquisite.

"Just grab a seat anywhere," our host insists. "The food is almost ready. Go ahead and sit down, and I'll bring the kabobs."

Later in the evening we discover that there are not just one but two full bathrooms in the man-cave, both of which feature small-screen televisions so you can refresh yourself without missing a moment of the televised action. Each bathroom is probably nine by twelve feet with floors of twenty-inch marble tile, laid diagonally. And this is the gazebo—we're not even in the sprawling house.

"This gazebo is larger than our whole house," David whispers to me while both of our hosts are retrieving food or drinks or dishes from somewhere else in the outdoor space. "This has to have two thousand square feet of covered space, maybe a bit more."

Our hosts return, and the four of us dine on succulent vegetables and perfectly braised chicken, skewered on metal rods that gleam like platinum. Is it even possible that skewers are made in such a precious metal? I decide to stop thinking about it. Throughout our dinner, both our host and hostess are animated and expressive, telling us about the trouble they had selling their previous home.

"We saw this place and had to have it," Jerry explains. "But it was almost eight months after we moved in here before we were finally able to sell our old place. Three separate deals fell through before that without reaching escrow."

We nod our heads appropriately, trying to seem distressed at the "troubles" our hosts suffered while moving from one mansion to the next. Meanwhile, the food and beverages keep coming.

I'm trying to calculate what this couple would have been paying on mortgages for two giant homes in the desert while they waited for one of them to sell. How much income would two jumbo-size mortgages eat up? These two definitely aren't Christian book authors, I decide.

At the couple's kind invitation, we've arrived 90 minutes before the basketball game begins, so we have plenty of time for a relaxed and delightfully entertaining meal. Our plates and glasses are quickly refilled before David or I have a chance to ask for seconds.

I am finishing my salad, pushing back from my second generously portioned kabob (I probably should have stopped at one), when Darlene gives me clear instructions about what to do next. She's glancing at me across the table, noticing that I'm slowing down.

"Lisa, you better save a little room yet. We've got kiwi and strawberries dipped in Belgian white chocolate. And Jerry wants to set something on fire for us later."

I look across at David, and he appears to read my mind.

Don't wake me, I'm thinking to myself. *I'm enjoying this dream too much!*

Snatching Work from the Jaws of Leisure

Later, we're sipping coffee and sampling white chocolate as game time nears.

Jerry rises and grabs a universal remote control device that looks more like an iPad. "I can control the whole house with this thing," he explains to us. "Lights, audio and video, climate control, security…I can even turn the waterfalls off and on."

He clicks on his largest outdoor television, we settle into the world's most comfortable leather chairs, and I take a sip of perfectly roasted decaf coffee. I've been married to David long enough to learn to enjoy Celtics basketball and become a fan in my own right. The NBA logo swells on the screen, and Kevin Garnett and the rest of the team walks to center court for the tip-off. And at *this* moment, our hostess, who has been happy and animated and relaxed all evening, rolls her eyes and asks her husband, "Do we really have to watch this right now?"

In a moment of sudden and shocked silence, everything is still in the man-cave. I can't speak for everyone in the room, but I thought all of us were planning on watching the game. Our invitation included it, and both Jerry and Darlene knew about our basketball preferences. They've been chattering about the Celtics since all of this came up as a possibility.

What is going on?

Darlene locks her husband into her direct gaze. "I was really hoping we could talk about our relationship tonight with David and Lisa," she continues in a half-whiny tone. "There's so much we need to work on, and how often do we get a chance to see these two? It's not often that we have professionals to talk to about our marriage issues."

I risk a sideways glance at my husband, who is outwardly serene, but I know that both of us are holding our breath at this moment. It is surreal. This close to a Celtics playoff game in this setting after a long weekend of work, and someone wants us to turn off the television and resume our role as family counselors?

Please, God, not right this moment. Can't we have a little time for us right now?

Jerry suddenly leans over like a deflated balloon. He crumples onto his chair, avoiding direct eye contact with Darlene. "I was really hoping we could just watch some basketball," he says quietly. "It's a playoff game after all, and it's the Celtics."

"All you ever want to do is watch sports," Darlene replies, her mouth forming the slightest hint of a disparaging sneer. "I thought at least this one time we could actually do some work on our marriage. Why am I the only one of us who wants to do that? Why is it always only me who wants our marriage to get better?"

The man-cave is deathly quiet. All of us can hear the burbling water outside and the distant whoosh of a jet passing somewhere overhead. David is staring at his hands, and I know he is praying. So am I. The room remains intensely still, and the atmosphere is completely different from what we experienced just a few moments ago, clustered around a bountiful dining table.

For several long seconds nobody speaks. Then Jerry reluctantly gives in without making a fight. "Okay," he tells his wife in a barely audible whisper. "If that's what you want to do tonight, that's what we'll do."

And with that, the Boston Celtics and the NBA playoffs disappear from the screen. Our working weekend in Phoenix gets a sudden and surprising Tuesday extension. *Okay, God, if this is what You really want, help us to get through this with grace and wisdom. Help us to be helpful here.*

The Volcano Erupts

In a split second, Darlene is off and running—not physically, but verbally. Now that she has permission to turn this evening of food and basketball into a counseling session, she forges ahead at full speed. She dominates the next 45 minutes, though David occasionally interjects and Jerry sometimes answers direct questions with short, quiet replies.

Darlene has a lot to say, and she seems to have been saving it for a moment like this. She spews out accusations like a volcano spitting hot lava. Apparently, for her, working on the relationship includes a large amount of time listening to her own voice, explaining her own perspective, and carefully pointing us to the solutions she believes are best.

We are amazed, not only that this is happening during a Celtics playoff game, but even more that she completely and constantly criticizes and condemns her husband, who is sitting only a few feet away from her and who agreed to alter the evening's plans.

David repeatedly interrupts our hostess, showing her how to change her direct attacks into less destructive and more useful "I feel" statements, but she consistently defaults to accusations and criticisms. She produces a long list of her husband's faults, sins, and defects, jumping from topic to topic and repeating herself often.

"All you do around here is watch sports."

"You care about football more than you care about me."

"You know more about Matt Leinart than you know about your own wife!"

"When you come home, you don't even look at me. You just look at the closest TV."

Darlene fires these criticisms at Jerry like tennis serves, sharp and quick. One after another, she finds ways to say essentially the same thing: Jerry is a slave to his sports instead of being an attentive, caring, and supportive life partner.

Is this the same husband who suddenly gave up a night of NBA playoff basketball so he could work on his marriage?

I begin to wonder if Darlene is trying to goad Jerry into something. Is she trying to provoke him to anger? Is she hoping he'll flare up and join the fighting? I sneak a glance at him, and he seems to be patiently enduring this tirade. But Darlene is just getting warmed up. She has even more issues to cover while the counselors are in the house. All of the topics of discussion revolve around her husband's alleged faults and failings.

Her criticism of him is constant; her tone of voice is accusing and judgmental. I can sense that our hostess is working her way up to the big stuff.

Let's Get Spiritual

Having attended one of the Sunday services in which David preached, and knowing that David is an ordained minister as well as a family counselor, Darlene now changes her approach and begins criticizing her husband for his spiritual faults and failings. Once again, her tone is strident and accusatory as she faces him.

"You're not the spiritual leader I always thought you would be."

"Why don't you spend as much time reading your Bible as you spend figuring out your fantasy football team?"

"Why am I always the one who wants us to get up and go to church on Sundays, but you seem like you never even want to go?"

"Our church has stuff for men all the time, and you never attend any of it. Why can't you at least go to a few of the men's Bible studies or men's prayer times? Why aren't you focused on God and His Word like the other men at church?"

"I thought I was marrying a spiritual man, but it turns out I was wrong. You don't even care about the things of God. All you care about is the NFL."

"I wanted to marry a man like my dad, someone who cared about God and who taught his family how to live the right way. Why can't you take the lead around here more often instead of always dragging your feet when I talk about church or God or spiritual things?"

"I never see you with a good devotional book in your hands. All I ever see you holding is that big remote control or a beer!"

Graciously, my husband—who was not expecting to be called into duty as a family counselor tonight—interrupts these outbursts to defuse the obvious attacks they contain. I'm proud of David as he consistently and firmly points Darlene back to healthy and useful ways to express her feelings. Each time he does, Darlene rephrases her statement. Even so, she is either a slow learner or simply refuses to back down. By the next verbal blast, she's forgotten the template and is back in attack mode. She seems unable or unwilling to learn. She rolls from attack to attack and from category to category. She is relentless. Hasn't anyone ever shown this woman how to explain herself using "I feel" statements?

Jerry makes very little effort to defend himself. I'm amazed by that. Most people get defensive when they're being attacked. First they raise their voices, and then they end up raising their own issues. Like the dueling couple in the old movie *Kramer vs. Kramer*, many wives and husbands end up ultimately dissolving their union because of a cycle of attacks and defenses. Combat generates tremendous damage and destroys relationships quicker than anything.

As Darlene makes more and more attacks, Jerry miraculously continues to make little effort to defend himself. Every once in a while, he interjects quietly to explain his own efforts.

"I went to that men's night at church that you signed me up for."

"I got a simpler translation of the Bible, and I think it's helping me understand things a little better."

"I'm sorry, but I work hard for us all week and don't always feel like jumping out of bed on Sunday morning, getting dressed up, and going to church."

"I do love God, but maybe I just don't express it the same way you do."

"I'm not comfortable standing up and praising God the way we do at church. I didn't grow up with that, and it seems kind of strange to me. It's fine for other people, but it's not something I can see myself doing."

"I don't like sharing my inner feelings with anyone, and definitely not other men."

Jerry quietly offers these explanations, not to win an argument, but to help his wife understand. I'm amazed. Although many people are on their best behavior around family counselors, this is an impressive display of restraint and goodwill.

I may seem to be taking sides, but I'm not. It's just that on this particular evening, with two out-of-state guests in her house, Darlene is in full attack mode. Miraculously, Jerry is avoiding the usual trap of getting defensive. Meanwhile, David walks a tightrope as he tries to guide the discussion in healthy and acceptable ways. Over and over again he patiently but firmly instructs Darlene how to make "I feel" statements and how to avoid making statements that attack or belittle another person.

She appears to be learning impaired.

"I really wasn't prepared for that," David tells me on our drive back to the hotel. "They never suggested having us over for a counseling session, which I'd be open to if they asked about it. Tonight was supposed to be food and basketball, and the whole evening really caught me off guard. I wasn't prepared for how it went."

I believe David did well under the circumstances, and I tell him so as we drive home. He reaches across the car to take my hand.

"Thanks for grading on the curve," he says with a wry smile, exhausted.

Death in the Desert: A Relationship Ebbs Away

Jerry and Darlene are smarter than average and much more prosperous than average, and they have attended church for most or all of their adult lives. They are spiritually literate and well educated. Their marriage, viewed from the outside, seems to be pretty normal. Their success, judged by the house and the cars and the furniture and the toys—is impressive. Yet underneath these outward appearances is a relationship that is starved for affection, intimacy, and depth. These two, married for almost two decades, have somehow managed to grow further and further apart. In our previous social encounters with them, we've not seen the trends that emerge so dangerously and in such unhelpful ways on this warm Arizona evening.

One of Jerry's revealing statements, very late in a long night of talking and listening and praying and helping, summarizes some of the core problems that trouble this particular home. It comes at a moment when Darlene is silent, having seemingly exhausted her energy in a tirade of attacks and criticisms and pointed comments. After a moment's silence, Jerry chooses his words carefully and cautiously.

"No matter what I do," he tells her, his voice quiet and his manner composed and gentle, "it seems like my effort doesn't get noticed. It seems like even when I do something, it's never the right thing. It's not good enough. Honestly, it seems like you don't even notice the progress I make sometimes or the good things I do. I'm never quite good enough. I can never be as godly as your dad or be the spiritual giant you want me to be. Maybe I just don't have what it takes. Maybe I'm just not that kind of person. When you tell me I'm failing, I just want to quit trying," he says softly. Unknowingly, he speaks for husbands all around the world.

Even as we hear Jerry's closing remark, David and I realize it would make a profound title for a book. "I just want to quit trying." This is how he feels when he's told he's a constant failure, that nothing he does ever measures up to Darlene's standards. Instead of earning points for his good behavior, he watches his ratings sink lower and lower.

Not good enough. Not often enough. Not attentive enough. Not godly enough.

Every time Jerry tries to change or improve, Darlene criticizes him. Like a gerbil running in a wheel, he races and races but never gets ahead. But unlike the gerbil, Jerry quickly realizes that his hard work will not be rewarded. So he makes the logical decision and quits trying.

The Power of Positive Reinforcement

Men need respect, which is one reason unemployment is so tough for males. Men often derive a lot of their respect from the jobs they do, the careers they build, the salaries they earn, or their professional accomplishments.

But husbands also need respect from their wives. Often, they receive that respect when the couple is courting. When a woman laughs at a man's jokes, compliments his wisdom, or praises his performance, she builds up his respect and meets one of his primary personal needs. Conversely, when these features are absent from a relationship, one of a male's most important needs is going unmet. When a husband's need for respect is not being fulfilled at home, he is more likely to explore other ways to earn the positive affirmation and personal encouragement he needs.

Why do men work so much? Often it's because the job site or the career is where the positive reinforcement occurs, where the self-esteem is built, and where the sense of worth and dignity is most established. The need for respect is hardwired into the male circuitry, so many males naturally get out of balance in the category of work and employment.

The reasons why men tend to work so much are varied and complex, but perhaps the simplest one is this: Success feels good. Earning a paycheck feels good. Providing for a family feels good. Owning a home feels good. And let's face it—if it feels good, men are ready to do it.

Respect, Motivation, and Effort

So what happens when a man finds respect on the job but comes home to a wife who does not seem to respect him? This is the situation David and I encounter on a sparkling clear night in Arizona. Jerry is making an effort to measure up, to achieve, and to earn his wife's respect. Yet instead of gaining that respect, he somehow loses points by trying. His best efforts and his most sincere attempts to change are rated as failures. Like the late comedian Rodney Dangerfield, this husband gets no respect.

How long will a typical male keep struggling in this environment, trying to earn the respect and approval of a nagging, critical wife who is never satisfied? The answer varies, but the general trend is clear enough: not very long.

Faced with a lack of respect at home, men will mentally check out. They may be physically present but maintain a highly separate emotional and personal life. They may work more hours, drink to excess, indulge in Internet pornography, or find excuses to be out of the house most of the day, coming home only to sleep and eat. If a man has parents or other relatives nearby, he may suddenly feel the need to volunteer to help them with chores, errands, and projects.

Patterns like these are typical indicators that a man does not feel respected at home. He isn't putting points on the board. Faced with a difficult or hostile environment in which to compete for the respect he needs, a man tends to gravitate to some other venue. The need for respect is so great that men will unconsciously prioritize tasks, situations, or environments from which they are likely to derive the most respect. If respect is available outside the home, that's where a man's attention and affections will focus.

When men don't put points on the board in one arena, they tend to change gymnasiums and play on a more friendly court. Or to use a golf analogy, men will look for a course with fewer sand traps and ponds and faster greens. They'll look for a course where they can succeed.

Men whose wives don't respect them are far more likely to engage in inappropriate relationships with coworkers, neighbors, or friends. The temptation to become emotionally attached to other women increases. They may spend hours on Facebook searching for old girl-friends or trying to make new ones.

Men are wired to achieve respect, and in a world where divorce is easy, new relationships are readily available, and "everyone's doing it," men are unlikely to remain in a setting where their basic need for respect is not being met.

This is not an excuse for male behavior, but an explanation of it.

Right Hopes, Wrong Approach

For Jerry and Darlene, barbecue night has arrived just in time. As we explore their relationship in a later appointment, we uncover why Darlene resorted to such unhelpful behavior. "I just wanted to get his attention," she says. "I thought if I showed him how poorly he was doing, I could motivate him to try harder and change. I kept yelling at him because I just didn't think he could hear me!"

From our perspective outside the relationship, we can easily see the foolishness of using behaviors and strategies that don't lead to positive change. And simply yelling louder will make the situation worse, not better.

Somehow Darlene doesn't notice that her behavior is deflating her husband's ego, sapping his motivation to try harder, and potentially even driving him into the arms of a more supportive, more encouraging new partner. Darlene means well, and she has the right hopes, but her nagging, attacking, criticizing, and condemning discourages Jerry and drains his motivation. She needs a U-turn in her speech and her behavior, which brings us to your turn.

Reflections for Your Personal Journey

1. Did Darlene's behavior remind you of yours? How?

2. Which do you do more often—praise your husband's behavior, compliment his appearance, and thank him for something he's done, or complain and criticize? Are you more likely to put him down or build him up? (See Ephesians 4:29.)

3. What would your words sound like to an outsider listening in? If you were recorded during the day, would the playback reveal a negative person or a positive person? Regardless of your motives and intentions, how do your words usually come out?

4. Is your husband's need for respect being met right now? How? Is he getting a lot of respect at work? Is he succeeding in his career? Is he receiving more appreciation and respect at home than anywhere else? How can you create a positive and encouraging environment so he feels respected and successful at home?

5. Have you noticed and commented on the positive things your husband does in your relationship? When he helps with the kids or does a project to improve your house, do you thank him and compliment him? Do you focus on what your husband doesn't get done, or are you grateful for the things he accomplishes?

6. When your husband comes home from playing basketball or golf or softball, do you listen to him or care how he played? When he achieves a new high score on his favorite video game, do you cheer for his accomplishment, or do you act as if playing video games is a childish waste of time?

7. When you talk about your husband with others, do they respect him more than they did before? How might your

words affect the way your friends, family, and children treat him?

8. When your husband is too tired to want sex, can you be okay with that? When he's in the mood and insistent, can you go along with it sometimes? In what ways can you let him lead more often, showing him your respect even in the timing and situations where intimacy occurs? In your busy life as a worker, wife, and mom, do you sometimes shut him out for your own convenience?

9. In a private session with a counselor, completely off the record, would your husband say he is respected at home? Why or why not?

When It's Better to Say
Nothing at All: Unhelpful Gossip

nstead of walking over to False Creek for a picnic, we're driving to the far slope of the mountains for some afternoon coffee. We won't be taking the water taxi to Granville Island today, splashing our way across a narrow band of waves. Instead, we'll voyage in our van through the leafy, forested contours of Stanley Park, crossing over the Lions Gate Bridge to North Vancouver. From there, we'll aim westward on the freeway for several kilometers, making our way to a suburban coffee shop located high on the hill across the bay.

It's a waste of petrol. We can walk to six different name-brand coffee stores from our short-term apartment, each one less than four blocks away. The dense core of Vancouver seems to have a Starbucks on every corner. Each has its own clientele, its own demographic, and its own aura. We've sampled all the brand-name and independent coffee shops within walking distance of our home away from home.

Through God's grace and a variety of online miracles, we're in Vancouver for the summer, squirreled away on the top floor of an urban high-rise. The condo is fully furnished and available to us all summer long. It's got secure, climate-controlled underground parking for our Honda Odyssey, and it's located within walking distance of museums, restaurants, great shopping, and yes, plenty of coffee. Good-bye, former world. Hello, British Columbia!

We have a few weddings to perform and a handful of speaking engagements we just can't bring ourselves to cancel, but aside from those, our sabbatical is dedicated to writing. Yet somehow, opportunities to counsel know how and where to find us. We're glad to be available, but we are reminded of the character Richard Dreyfus plays in one of our favorite movies, *What About Bob?* Dreyfus, who plays a somewhat inept counselor, just wants to get away for some vacation. But for whatever reason, his wife, his kids, the operators at his phone service, and the other key people in his life just don't seem to understand that he needs some time off.

We can relate.

Our Working Vacation Continues

We've agreed to counsel a young couple over late-afternoon coffee. We met them while visiting a church the previous Sunday. We liked both of them immediately—so earnest, so sincere, so evidently serious about making the world a better place.

"They're both wound a little tight," David observes after we meet them. "Maybe we should give them our sabbatical while we take over their teaching chores for a while. What do you think?"

Our two new friends are both teaching for the summer. He's leading a graduate course at a highly respected Christian university. She's teaching English as a second language. They seem delightfully compatible. Both of them are obviously highly intelligent and claim to enjoy teaching. But generally speaking, when you make an appointment to see a counselor, you probably aren't planning to trade recipes or talk about the weather.

As we drive to our appointment, the forest of high-rise buildings gives way to actual trees. Stanley Park, much like Central Park in New York, is an oasis of green in the midst of a bustling, densely packed city. The transition into park space is visually stunning and immediately refreshing. We've traded concrete for grass, flower boxes in windows for beautiful clusters of roadside wildflowers.

"Let's have lunch here tomorrow," David suggests as we round a corner to discover a picnic area shaded under centuries-old trees. "We could grab some Subway and come out here for the early afternoon."

Traffic moves slowly but steadily through the park. In due course we come to a turn lane that leads to the Lion's Gate Bridge. A few moments later we are high above the bay, with spectacular views below us and all around us. Above us the rocky peaks are lined with snow along the upper ridges. We can see trickles of waterfalls here and there in the lower elevations.

Vancouver is paradise, regardless of what the locals may tell you.

We are smack in the center of the bridge's long span when a classic floatplane soars right over us. Traffic is slow, and we can watch the plane's lazy arc through the afternoon sky. The buzz of the motor sounds erratic and tentative to our ears, but perhaps it's normal for smaller aircraft. Is he planning to land that plane on the roof of our van?

Across the bridge we are busy looking for signs that will point us toward West Vancouver. We've been here before but not frequently. We remember a dazzling view of Stanley Park from high above the city. Just moments from now, we'll see it again as we chase along the freeway toward Exit 7.

When we reach the exit, we are still almost 15 minutes early for our appointment. "Let's look at some houses," David suggests, and we spend the first 10 minutes driving through nearby neighborhoods and watching for brochures and for-sale signs.

We follow a sharp curve on a steep downhill bend, round a corner, and both let out the same expressive sigh. Before us is a 180-degree view of the city and the bay, with Stanley Park in the foreground. In a life of traveling and sightseeing and exploring, this is one of the most beautiful vistas we've discovered. Both of us are silent for a moment.

"We're moving here," my husband tells me quietly, only half kidding.

"I'm already packed," I reply, grinning.

Our destination is a U-shaped strip mall with interesting stores and, we later discover, the best dry cleaners in the Vancouver metro. We make note of a machine that will recycle the cans and bottles we've been saving all summer. We find the Starbucks nestled in the base of the mall's U, facing back toward the east. Although we can't see the bay from here, rocky slopes and tall trees are visible and scenic. The outdoor tables feature leaf-framed mountain views.

David parks the van, and we're quickly in the door of the coffee shop with plenty of time to check the menu and hunt for a quiet table. Our new friends aren't here yet, but they'll be punctual, arriving exactly on time.

"Would you like a sample of biscotti?" a smiling barista asks me.

Is there an A *in Canada?* I think to myself, simply nodding yes.

David says yes to a sample also and then passes me his. This is one of the advantages of being happily married.

Canadian Body Language, Eh?

Happily married or not, the couple we're meeting comes through the door of Starbucks wearing worried expressions. We can read their moods from across the room. Jarrod and Melody both seem a little bit tense, a little bit on edge. This doesn't seem like an auspicious beginning for our time together.

Seeing us, Melody smiles quickly. "There you are!" she exclaims as they rush to our side. "We were worried that we told you to drive east on the 1 instead of west," she explains. "When we got here, both of us wondered if we'd given you wrong directions."

"No worries," David assures the couple. "We had no trouble at all finding the place." His statement is true and seems to have a calming effect.

"Oh, good," Melody says, visibly slumping a bit.

"We were worried," Jarrod adds, stating the obvious.

Twenty minutes later we haven't done any counseling yet, but we've heard how they met, their wedding stories, and some of their personal histories. So far the conversation has been positive, romantic, and memorable. Nothing has set our internal alarm bells jangling.

Counseling couples for a living, we often tiptoe through some of the fields we encounter, not knowing where land mines may be buried. Here and now, sipping coffee and talking about weddings and honeymoons and world travel, we don't feel the need to be quite so wary.

David often has people begin conversationally like this so they are relaxed when we finally arrive at the difficult work. Jarrod and Melody are visibly less stressed than they appeared when they walked in. He is animated and expressive and highly verbal. She adds color commentary and only occasionally corrects him. At this early stage of our time together, her temperament appears generally positive and optimistic. She seems surprisingly free and easy when raising potentially sensitive topics—a fact that leads to the core of the couple's problem.

An Exit Ramp Marked Shame

"We didn't really leave Boise by choice," Jarrod says as he begins to tell us his view of their core issue. "It got so we just couldn't live there anymore."

This gripping introduction immediately attracts our attention. What has transpired that forces this nice young couple to leave their home? Why are they no longer welcome in one of Idaho's finest cities?

David interrupts to clarify a point. "Excuse me—couldn't live there anymore, or didn't want to live there anymore?" he asks, his gaze fastened directly on Jarrod.

"Well, uh…didn't want to I guess," Jarrod replies. "I mean, things had just gotten way too difficult. It just wasn't possible to…"

He lets his sentence drift into space, and no one completes his thought. A few moments go by without further comment from anyone.

"So the purpose of our meeting with you today is to hear about the reason you left Boise?" David eventually inquires with candor, directness, and gentle kindness. "Is that the main thing we're considering today?"

Jarrod and Melody nod, almost in unison.

"Yes, that's it," she says. "And I'm afraid of starting the whole crazy pattern all over again way up here. I don't want to do that. I don't want to spend our lives on the move."

"I don't want that either," her husband agrees.

Gossip Makes the World Go Round

As we begin hearing about this couple's harmful habit, we immediately recognize it from other counseling sessions. It's a temptation that far too many young wives succumb to. Although the details vary from person to person and from couple to couple, the pattern is similar in many early marriages.

The new wife, feeling a bit lonely or reaching out for some fresh friendship, shares some personal details about her husband or her marriage. These details circulate into a church, office, neighborhood, circle of friends, or family, where they weaken respect for the husband. If the pattern continues, the husband begins to feel threatened in many of his usual social settings. He may withdraw, isolate, or—in cases such as the one we're hearing today—even insist that the couple move to a new location and start over. The reasons vary, but the pattern is clear.

"I came home one day, and he was watching porn on TV," Melody begins bluntly. Jarrod visibly squirms in front of us, but to his credit, he doesn't speak. Obviously he's heard this before and knows where this conversation is going. Melody continues her narrative.

"I got home earlier than I usually do and walked into our living room, and there he was with all these naked cheerleaders, or whatever they were, all over our TV screen. We had spent way too much money on way too large of a television set, and now the whole wall of my living room was covered with breasts that were also way too large. I mean, no one has breasts that size, at least not in real life!"

Jarrod is completely silent. I look around the coffee shop to see if our conversation is attracting other listeners. Too-large breasts are definitely of compelling interest to some people. But no one seems to be listening in on our conversation. God bless these discreet Canadians.

Melody gets back to her story. "I didn't know whether to yell at him, or cry, or what. I was just so shocked by it. You don't expect to walk into your living room at two or three in the afternoon and find a bunch of giant breasts waving around on your TV screen!"

Jarrod stares down into his coffee. Meanwhile, David is swirling a plastic spoon in his drink, not looking at Melody but indicating to her by his body language that he is listening and attentive.

"So what started it, for me, was this big shock at home," Melody explains. "Nothing had really prepared me for this."

Pay No Attention to That Porn on the Big Screen

"That isn't really our problem." This is Jarrod's first statement since the beginning of this topic of discussion. "I mean, it's a problem of course, but it's not why we left Boise, and it's not why we came here today."

He looks around the room somewhat nervously before going on. "I was studying really hard, working on my doctorate and teaching some courses, and my brain was kind of fried. I just wanted to relieve some of my built-up tension. So I sat down at the TV that afternoon, planning to watch some sports or something. I was just flipping through the channels.

"I didn't really sit down that day to watch a bunch of naked women—honest, I didn't—but when they came on, it was kind of interesting. I mean, at that point Melody and I hadn't had sex in like a month or more because of our different schedules. So in my own defense, looking at a naked woman was kind of appealing."

Now it's Melody's turn to say nothing. I wonder what she is thinking. Meanwhile, David, always gracious but also unfailingly direct, has decided to begin his cross-examination.

"It's kind of interesting that you bring up a problem like pornography but also tell us that it's not the main problem."

David neither explains nor continues this statement. He just lets his words hang out in space for a moment. It's a technique he often uses with great effect.

The husband is back-pedaling in a hurry. "Well, yeah…as I said, pornography is a problem—of course it is! It's just not a problem for us. I don't watch that kind of stuff. The one time it does come on and I don't turn it off is the one time Melody comes home, walks in, and sees it. What are the odds of that happening? I mean, it's not like it was something I was into at the time. It's not something I'm into now. I don't want to look at pictures of naked women I don't even know. What I want to do is make love to my wife in the real world. That whole thing with the TV was just one moment in a long day in a long season of grading papers and writing papers and being married but not getting any of the benefits of being married, and it all built up, and yes, when I saw the naked women, I knew I shouldn't watch, but I did anyway."

Jarrod pauses, seemingly out of breath. Is it just me, or is he maybe protesting a bit too much?

"So do I have to pay for one stupid mistake the rest of my life?" he asks us with a shrug. "That's the problem, or it's sort of the problem, we want to talk with you about."

Jarrod seems to have run out of words. He sits back in his chair, tips his coffee cup up to his mouth, and realizes that he is not only out of words but also out of warm caffeine.

The Benefit of the Doubt

When Melody speaks, her voice is almost a whisper. "I believe him. I should have believed him sooner. But at that time in our marriage, finding my husband in the living room with a TV full of naked women—I just didn't know how to handle that! It just really rocked my world. It was the last thing on earth I expected to find. Both of us are young, both of us are healthy and attractive…okay, we hadn't had sex recently, but in general we had a good sex life going. So I didn't see any reason at all why Jarrod would be sitting there drooling in front of the TV set with these gigantic fake breasts parading all over the screen."

She is working her way up to something, but we don't know what.

"Anyway," she says finally, after another long pause, "that's why I was so shocked and didn't know how to handle things. That's why it had such a big impact on me. And I guess I didn't make very good choices. I see that now. My response wasn't helpful—I get that. But I'm afraid it's so much a part of who I am, and the way I am…I'm afraid this is going to keep being a problem if we don't get a handle on it soon!"

She hasn't told us the problem yet, but we're getting there.

Have You Heard the Latest?

"Melody started talking about me to other people," Jarrod says. "I guess she was surprised or worried or upset, but she told her best girlfriend at church what happened. And that girlfriend told the wife of one of our other friends, and before I knew what was going on, everybody at church was giving me these strange looks as if I were some kind of a pervert.

"One friend—the husband of Melody's best girlfriend there— came up to me at church, and he's like, 'Dude, you are so busted!' and he started to laugh."

Jarrod is animated and looking right at David. "I don't even do pornography. I'm not into that kind of stuff, and then the next thing I know, this guy at church who has been my friend is kidding me about being a perv! And he thinks it's funny somehow, like everybody does it, but the smart ones don't get busted by their wives in the middle of the afternoon! And did I mention that this conversation is happening right there in the church parking lot?"

Jarrod is speaking rapidly. His face is flushed. Clearly this topic raises strong emotions in him. He is also getting gradually louder. As he says "perv," I notice a glance from across the room. Our open-air counseling session may not be quite so private anymore.

Exhausted from talking about it, Jarrod falls silent, and no one jumps in to begin a new topic. Maybe the people across the room will lose interest in this line of discussion. Sipping the remnants of a decaf grande soy latte, no foam, I certainly hope so.

A Confidence Spirals out of Control

"It wasn't just at church," Melody admits after we've sat together in silence for a few moments. "I talked about it to other people too. I had a long conversation with my older sister, and then she went and told my mom. Can you believe that? I mean, I have no idea why she thought that was appropriate to tell my mother.

"Next thing I know, my mom is on the phone telling me that if I'm being abused at home or if there is bad stuff going on, I don't have to stay with Jarrod. She's basically telling me it's okay to leave my husband." Melody pauses, clearly distraught.

"At the time, it seemed completely okay to trust my sister because I was newly married and didn't expect to find my man doing porn. I just reached out to my older sis for help because she's been married longer and I thought she would understand. And the next thing I know, she's telling my mom, and my mom is yelling at me on the phone, and my husband's reputation is ruined in our family."

Melody has mother issues, but her primary focus is elsewhere.

"So it wasn't just at church that I messed up. I told some of my Facebook friends about it, but I tried to use code and sort of talk about it without saying it for real. But I guess I wasn't so clever in my fake words. So people on Facebook figured it out. I took down two whole posts about it, but it was already too late. My wall got lots of stuff written on it, some of which was not appropriate at all.

"I ruined our whole life because I was scared and confused and I didn't know what to do. So I ran to my girlfriend and my sister, and I almost lost my marriage. I was so stupid!"

I like Melody already, and I completely sympathize with her situation. However, right now, she just seems to want attention. I get the feeling she's fishing for sympathy and wanting affirmation. I think about speaking up ever so briefly but decide to let her keep fishing. But I do care about her situation, and I'll take the time later to assure her that whatever else may be true, she is certainly not stupid. I'd give that award to the guy watching the big boobs on his big TV screen. He's the next person to speak.

"Anyway, now I guess you know why we left Idaho. Melody's family and all our closest friends were right there, and I just couldn't walk into church and look at any of them after that. I couldn't go to family gatherings anymore. We went to Melody's dad's birthday right after all this happened, and her dad was totally glaring at me the whole night. I kept expecting him to drag me upstairs and tell me I was grounded! Maybe it would have been better if he had said something, but he didn't. He just glared at me with this really mean stare for the whole evening. I felt like he was saying 'I knew you shouldn't have married my daughter! I knew you weren't good enough for her! I knew you were a total pervert!'"

Jarrod continues after a brief pause. "I couldn't wait for us to get out of there that night. I couldn't wait to leave Melody's parents' house and just drive home. I felt so ashamed, so disrespected...I just wanted to die right then and there. I kept thinking that if I died right then, maybe they would at least say nice things about me at my funeral. No matter what you do in your life, people have to say nice things about you at your funeral! I just wanted to die."

Jarrod looks down at the floor. Okay, I decide, both of them want attention. Maybe that's why they sought us out after a church service a few days ago.

I notice that David is not rushing in with any quick affirmations either. After a pause in which no one speaks at all, Jarrod resumes his story.

"So anyway, now you know what our real problem is. I do not have an issue with pornography. We made sure that we didn't get any premium channels when we moved up here to Vancouver. We don't even have HBO or Showtime right now. We only have basic cable with one sports package on it. But I'm afraid if there's any kind of a problem in our marriage, or if I do any little thing wrong or make some kind of mistake, I'm going to turn around and find out that the whole world already knows about it. I'm afraid that the next time I screw something up, everyone is going to be laughing at me."

His voice trails off into silence, and the four of us settle in for a 90-minute discussion of the main topic of this chapter: the devastatingly negative power of unhelpful gossip, especially when a wife is talking about her husband.

Yes We Do Discuss These Other Matters

For the record, we should clarify that David had a chat with Jarrod about pornography. Before leaving this couple, we split up and worked man-to-man and woman-to-woman for a few minutes.

"I wanted to deal with that issue in private," David tells me later. "I got very direct with him and asked him quite a few questions I wouldn't have raised at the table with all four of us there. I think he's being straight with me. I think his incident of being caught actually scared him out of further involvement with porn. He seemed honest and remorseful about ever having gone there in the first place.

"As far as I can tell," David says, "he doesn't have an ongoing problem in that area. It appears to have been an aberration, based on going quite a while without normal sexual activity with his wife. He was home alone and made some unwise entertainment choices, but he seems to have learned from that mistake."

So now, let's return to the primary topic of our chat with Jarrod and Melody. Of all the pitfalls and traps that can snag an unwary wife, gossip is especially damaging. As we have already seen, a husband's sense of well-being is tied to his need for respect.

If a husband is out of work, his physical and emotional health is likely to suffer. One of his primary sources of respect is missing, and consequences are bound to arise. A husband whose wife undermines him with others is vulnerable in the same way. As he loses other people's respect, his own self-esteem may plummet, with physical and emotional repercussions.

This is why it is so extremely damaging when wives share negative or critical information about their husbands with others (even when it's true). You can make your girlfriend promise not to tell, but she's likely to talk about it with at least one other person, maybe more. You can expect your sister to exercise good discretion, but the next thing you know, she's calling your mom and explaining your business.

A lot of young wives have learned this. Maybe their example can help you avoid this common mistake. The problem with confiding in people is this: You have no idea whom *they* plan to confide in, and before you know it, a string of gossip is set in motion, one conversation at a time.

A Time and a Place to Discuss Problems

Sensitive and negative details about your husband are not items you should release into the information stream. Rather than finding this out the hard way, consider in advance whether you should share personal matters and with whom. If you're looking for discretion, paid professional counselors and ministers are two of the best places to turn.

Counselors and pastors hear difficult and damaging information every day. They keep it to themselves, they don't post it on Facebook, and they don't call your mother. You can even ask them not to take written notes. David, since his early graduate school days, has never kept written notes or computer files of his counseling sessions for precisely that reason.

"How would you feel," David asked when we first talked about this, "if you knew that your worst secrets were written in someone's notebook or stored away on someone's computer? Even if you trust that person, how do you know where his notebook might end up some day? How do you know who may get unauthorized access to that computer file?"

You can ask your counselor or pastor not to take notes. It's not an unusual request. If you'd be more comfortable not having a written record, say so up front. Make sure that the counselor or pastor is willing to respect your wishes.

You may have heard stories of pastors and their wives not being trustworthy, but those are clearly rare exceptions. Day in and day out, pastors deal with some of life's most difficult issues and complicated problems with complete confidentiality. If your pastor is a male and you're not comfortable speaking with a male about a certain topic, find out if his wife takes appointments and meets with women for prayer or advice. Quite often this is the case. Or your church may have another woman in leadership who fills this role, offering confidential counsel and useful prayer support.

Does the Whole World Need to Know?

We could easily devote a whole book to the dangers of pornography, and perhaps one day we will. David has counseled with many husbands, including pastors, to help them overcome addictions to Internet or other pornography. He's worked with male sex addicts in a variety of counseling environments and in Celebrate Recovery meetings. Sexual addictions and involvement in porn are also becoming more common among women. But for now, let's say you're a wife who just caught her husband viewing pornography.

What's happening in that moment? For one thing, you are losing respect for your husband. You're worried, you're upset, you're possibly afraid, and even though you know his many good qualities and his many fine character traits, you've lost some of the respect you once had for your life partner and friend. So consider the likelihood that anyone you talk to about this will also lose some respect for the man you married. The more damaging or sensitive or negative the information, the more likely it is that anyone you talk to will lose respect for him. In a very short time, an entire family or congregation can change their opinion about someone, all because you didn't keep things confidential.

Is this an outcome that you're trying to create? God forbid.

In a difficult situation, if you feel lost and worried and you really want help, seek it where it can best be found. Turn to a professional counselor or a member of the clergy and speak with him or her honestly and in complete confidence. Pastors and priests and rabbis know a lot of negative things about a lot of people, and in general our ministers find a way to respect us even when we mess up. Clergy members and counselors are good at that because they have to practice it all the time. They seem to realize that people are imperfect and that struggles are normal and expected. They also know how to help.

Easy to Break, Impossible to Fix

If you damage your husband's reputation at church or in your family, repairing his social standing later may be difficult or even impossible. Saying something in an unguarded moment is all too easy. Repairing the damage later is not always an option, regardless of what you say or how you say it. By then, it's usually too late.

Think about it in another context. If you found out that one of the leaders in your church had a problem with pornography, would you vote for him to serve on the elder board? Once you learned that a man in your congregation spent his time looking at pictures of nude women, would you still feel comfortable when you were around him socially or in a worship setting? Let's face it, the things we learn about people tend to affect our respect for them for a long time. This happens even at the subconscious level.

Yes, churches should be places of forgiveness. But no, church people do not forget as easily as they try to forgive. This is why some people change churches or move out of town. Once a reputation is soiled, restoring it is nearly impossible. The person's name will always have an asterisk by it (figuratively speaking). Maybe things shouldn't be this way, but this is exactly how things are. Once a person's reputation is damaged, he has little hope of being respected as he once was.

Reputations are easy to break and sometimes almost impossible to repair. And this is why you should talk about the tough stuff with a paid counselor or a minister or the spouse of a minister. You should ask for and receive assurances that anything you say will be kept in strict confidence.

Your friends and siblings are undoubtedly wonderful people, but are they good at keeping secrets and never betraying your confidence? Sharing unhelpful gossip about your husband (even if the facts of the story are true) is a terrible way to find out that your sister, your best friend, or your coworker cannot actually be trusted to keep a secret.

If you'd like to avoid having to move away from your friends and family, try keeping private matters in private places. Trust the trustworthy and guard your conversations with all others.

Jarrod and Melody's story takes a happy turn several years later when we encounter them at a leadership conference. They rush up to greet us, all smiles, acting as if they've never had a problem in the world.

"I want to thank you so much for talking with us that day," Melody says to me in the crowded aisle of a megachurch gymnasium. "I just want you to know, I really took your words to heart. I haven't been sharing any gossip about my husband with my family, my friends... not anyone. I've really learned to watch the content of my conversation. If I'm not building him up, I just shut up!"

Remarkably sage advice, and it comes from the voice of experience. Keeping your confidential matters in trustworthy, confidential places will make your own life better and will guard the reputation of the man you married.

A Little Balance Here, Please

One other note. We are not saying you need to guard the reputation of a scoundrel or protect someone who is actively harming you or others. Sometimes the worst thing you could possibly do is keep silent! You do not need to hide the harm you or others are experiencing. Get to a safe place, speak up, and protect yourself.

Yet even in these extreme cases, the solution to the problem is not to start spreading gossip or stirring up negative conversation among your family or your friends. Confine these confidential matters to confidential places. Think before you speak.

That's what this chapter is saying to you—not to cover up for a husband who is abusing you and causing you harm, but rather to reveal something negative about your husband only in the right place. Choose your audience carefully, knowing the lasting damage that unhelpful gossip causes. Before you ruin the reputation of another person, stop and make wise choices about who to confide in.

A Biblical Perspective on Our Words

Ephesians 4:29 puts it wisely: "Do not use harmful words, but only helpful words, the kind that build up and provide what is needed." Although the context of this verse is not directly aimed at marriages, it certainly applies. Building up your husband will bring great rewards in the future. Tearing down your husband may cause great and enduring harm.

Once you've told a harmful story about someone else, once you've damaged his or her reputation, you may have broken something that is difficult or impossible to repair. You may never again be able to restore a relationship or enjoy a family circle that is healthy and happy. So think before you speak. And if what you're sharing is negative or will harm a reputation, find a confidential place for that revelation.

Avoid the damage that unhelpful gossip can do. When you talk about your husband with your friends, your mom, your coworkers, or someone at a ladies' luncheon in your church, speak positively and help other people gain more respect for the man you married.

Reflections for Your Personal Journey

1. Think about some of your closest married girlfriends. How do they talk with you about their husbands? Do you have a friend who frequently shares negative information about her husband? Is your friend gaining or losing by indulging in this kind of behavior? Why does she do this?

2. If you recorded every word that came out of your mouth, would you end up with negative comments about your husband? Have you talked with anyone recently who really didn't need to hear this kind of unhelpful gossip about your spouse?

3. Can your husband trust you to keep his bad habits, stupid ideas, or other minor failures away from the curious ears of family and friends? Or should he be worried every time you're out with your friends or at a women's Bible study?

4. What advice would you have given Melody when she came home and found Jarrod looking at other women's breasts on TV? Do you think she overreacted, or do you think she should set her husband out by the curb on trash day? What was your response to this story?

5. What is the difference between protecting your husband's privacy and reputation on one hand, and on the other, covering up for a man who is hitting or harming you? Are you clear on the fact that no one is asking you to remain in an abusive situation or hide your bruises? While we are talking about guarding reputations, be sure to guard yourself against being harmed or hurt. Please!

6. Would your parents say their respect for your husband has increased since you got married? Decreased? Why is their respect changing in this direction? Are you helping your family be proud of the man you married, or are you

causing your family to disrespect and possibly even dislike your life partner?

7. Do you understand why the husband in this chapter wanted to move away from Boise as quickly as possible? Do you understand how he felt attending his own church and being around his wife's family once other people knew about his mistake? Regardless of how you may feel about what he did, do you understand how he felt later around others?

8. Do you know a person who tends to gossip? All of us know such people. They're at the office, they're at church, and they live in the neighborhood. How can you avoid their gossip? Can you remember to speak more positively when you're in the company of someone who tends to gossip?

9. Make a list of trustworthy places you could go if you needed to have a confidential discussion. Sit down with a church directory or the Yellow Pages, or go online and look up counselors. Remind yourself of the resources that are readily available to you, right where you live, if you ever needed to discuss something in confidence.

10. As much as possible, can you make it your goal to improve other people's reputations rather than damage them? Can you especially focus on improving your husband's reputation? Can you build him up, encourage him, and cause others to look at him with new and increased respect?

6

The Elephant in the Room: Unresolved Bitterness

We're southbound on West River Road on a perfect October day in Minneapolis. The well-manicured lawns along the parkway are still wearing the greens and browns of the late summer season instead of the white overcoats of early winter. The sun overhead is absolutely brilliant. Fifty degrees is moderate for Minnesota, and we're grateful for the reprieve from the cold.

A steady stream of bicyclers passes us going north. They are pedaling mostly uphill but seem unfazed. Minnesotans, like Californians, are among the most healthy and active adult citizens of the United States. Locals here love their exercise and especially value being outdoors when conditions make it possible. According to an old joke on the northern plains, summer is beautiful, so come see it when it happens every fourth of July.

Traveling for a book event, we feared facing snow and ice along the streets of the Twin Cities metro area. Instead, we discover weather and culture that seem much more like early spring. Everyone is outdoors, walking or biking and enjoying the bright sun and the relative lack of wind. "It's the wind that gets to you," locals tell us about the winters here. "If it wasn't for the wind you could be outdoors at ten below zero and not really worry about it all that much."

We lived here for a decade, so we know better. We were doing community development, living and working in a gritty and crime-ridden neighborhood in the decaying core of Minneapolis. We formed and deepened some of our closest relationships during those years of hardship and struggle and ministry.

Hand in hand, together with students and young adults (at first we were the only married couple among the core of workers in our neighborhood), we watched God carve out a community of faith in a place that greatly needed His light. One by one we watched adults, teens, and children discover faith in Christ, find hope for a better future, and learn practical skills for living a healthy and wise life.

Those years—essentially for us the entire decade of the '90s—framed a lot of our theology and informed our approach to marriage therapy and family counseling. We left behind the comfortable suburbs and typical upper-middle-class problems, trading our own home and car for substandard housing and a rusty station wagon that became the free, always available community bus.

We were young and idealistic. Everything we attempted took longer than we expected. For the first three years we saw so little numerical growth that we often felt like failures in our ministry roles. Yet by the time we completed our mission and passed the torch to brighter and more capable workers, we had grown to love urban ministry. We also developed a deep and lasting affection for urban residents and for any and all places where the community of faith is multicultural—just like heaven will be.

Today, as we drive the tree-lined parkway through far better neighborhoods than the one we served while here, reminders of our Minnesota days come flooding back to us. We treasure these memories, and somehow even our failures seem poignant now. We regard even our setbacks and struggles with the warm affection of retrospect. Those were good times.

Deep below our road's pathway, a river gurgles downhill toward a high dam. We pass bridges, some old and some new, that link neighborhoods in southern Minneapolis with their counterparts in eastern St. Paul, divided by the river's flow.

As our drive began, we passed through much of the University of Minnesota campus, which sits on both banks of the river and thus occupies real estate in both of the Twin Cities. A pedestrian bridge, multiple bike lanes, and a busy freeway connect the two sides of the U of M campus, East Bank and West Bank.

Today, southbound in a rented Mitsubishi SUV, we've departed early so we can enjoy this journey. We pass an elementary school where I once served daily breakfast and lunch to urban children, many of whom qualified for free food service. For me, although the health insurance benefits and a school-season paycheck were part of the package, my time at the elementary school was about ministry to children and families. I miss those kids, especially in September's back-to-school flurry of activity.

Close Encounters of the First Kind

We're on our way to Caribou Coffee to meet a woman we don't yet know. She's not among our contacts from the community development days, and she didn't attend the church we helped plant in Beltrami Park. She is a referral from some of the ministry we've had recently at a megachurch in the Twin Cities, a vibrant congregation that has planted daughter churches in a wide radius across the metropolitan area.

Working with marriages and families brings us into constant contact with people who have friends, neighbors, coworkers, and family members "who really need to talk to someone right now." As people discover who we are and what we do for a living, almost everyone we meet talks about possibly referring someone to us. Many of those conversations result in referrals and counseling times. Quite a few of those sessions that begin as counseling times develop into lasting and meaningful friendships that we treasure and value over the course of many years.

It will happen to us today, although we don't know it yet.

We can see the skeletal outline of the Ford plant jutting skyward across the river as we near our intended bridge. For as long as we can remember, this plant has been turning out Ford Ranger pickup trucks and winning quality awards. It is consistently among the highest rated automotive production plants in North America. Still, rumors have often swirled here that the plant's closing is imminent.

Looking at rows of pickups in the parking lot, we can tell that despite a decade or more of rumors, the plant is still operating. That's good news for the auto workers of St. Paul and Minneapolis and for their families. With unemployment rates near all-time highs, we rejoice with anyone who has a job, and we pray for our many friends who don't.

David aims our hunter green Mitsubishi Endeavor across the high bridge, and we notice that a former favorite coffee and dessert venue called Bakers Square is still thriving. There are no Bakers Square outlets anywhere near our home in Southern California. Suddenly I'm hungry for French Silk pie, and David can almost taste a bacon and cheese omelet. Yet duty calls, and we drive onward to Caribou.

Caribou Coffee is a local chain that began as one couple's dream of smaller, more intimate coffee venues. Their business grew, they kept expanding, and now Caribou is scattered across Minnesota and growing rapidly in the Chicago metro. We delight when our air travels take us through airport locations that feature Caribou outlets. Caribou specialties include some hot cocoa concoctions that simply aren't available anywhere else.

Only a Caribou will do.

The parking lot is busy here. Caribou shares its parking spaces with an upscale grocery store, a bagel bakery, and a variety of other businesses that all appear to be thriving. We're glad for the higher sightlines and better visibility that come from our tall four-wheel-drive vehicle. Yet even with that advantage, we drive in circles for a while, struggling to find a place to park.

By the time we locate a parking space, which is nowhere near the entrance to Caribou but is clearly the best we're going to get, our counseling appointment is nearly due to begin. Despite our best efforts, we've squandered every minute of our margin on the scenic drive along the river, with detours through a few favorite neighborhoods and places. We walk in the door of Caribou Coffee precisely on time, which is about ten minutes later than our preferred and established pattern. Sharon, the woman we're meeting, is already seated and sipping her coffee. She waves at us across a crowded dining room. "I'm over here!" she says, smiling broadly.

As we arrive at her table she thrusts a $10 bill into our hands. "This one is on me," she insists as my husband politely declines her offer. After a few back-and-forth exchanges David agrees to allow our new friend to buy our coffee. It's the only fee we'll be charging today, and technically we didn't charge this either. We came to this meeting prepared to buy our own caffeine and some for our counselee also.

My So-Called Husband

Ten minutes later we are fully engaged in Sharon's story. Married for eight years, she's watched her husband morph from a romantic and attentive "good catch" to a lazy, perpetually unemployed, beer-drinking lout. He shows no interest in leaving the marriage, but he also shows absolutely no interest in making it better. He's content as things are. If Sharon's narrative is accurate, her husband lies around the house all day, drinks to excess, and claims to be looking for work. Meanwhile, she earns a living, pays the bills, and manages the household.

"Every mortgage payment in the past three years has come from my salary," she tells us. "Even when he was working somewhere, he'd cash his paycheck on the way home and start drinking it away, right then and there. If I didn't have my job [she's a loan officer at a local bank], we wouldn't have been able to keep this house. I've been wanting to quit working and start a family, but obviously that doesn't make any sense. If I did quit my job, we'd have no income, and pretty soon we wouldn't have a roof over our head. So I feel trapped in this whole thing."

We interrupt to ask about the early years of their relationship, and our new friend describes that season of her life.

"I was seventeen when we met," she begins. "He was four years older, very handsome…a real charmer. We started dating even though my mother didn't like him. By the time we had dated steadily for several months, I knew I wanted to marry him and spend the rest of my life with him."

"Before you tell us about your romance and marriage," David asks gently, "may we hear a bit more about your family of origin? Can you tell us about your home life while you were growing up?"

The woman nods at us quickly. "I guess I shouldn't be surprised that you picked up on that," she tells us. "Family life was very dysfunctional for me. My mom and my dad were never legally married. By the time I was old enough to know and remember people, my dad had already split. I didn't meet him until I was thirteen, and that was just a quick moment to say hi. He said he'd send me some money for my next birthday, but he never did.

"My mom never married, but there was almost always a man in the house. I grew up having temporary dads who stayed anywhere from a few weeks to a few months. In one case my mom was with a guy for almost five years. For a little while we almost felt like a family. But it eventually fell apart like all the others.

"I remember watching my mom—I was twelve or thirteen, just becoming a woman—I remember watching her and thinking, *I don't want to be anything like her. I want to be the opposite of that.*

"Mom was good looking and still is. She had me when she was fourteen, so she's only forty now. She never has any trouble getting a guy's attention. She still seems to be able to walk into a room, or usually a bar, and walk out with a guy.

"So, anyway, I guess my answer is getting kind of long. My birth dad has never been a part of my life. For the longest time I wanted a stepdad who would be there for me like a father would, but that never really happened.

"The guy who stayed with my mom for five years…I kind of liked him, but he didn't really get involved with me or my brother. He wasn't emotional or affectionate or anything, at least not with us. He spent a lot of time in front of the TV and in his bedroom.

He didn't really do things with me or with my little brother. I give him credit for staying with my mom for so long, and it's the closest we ever came to being a real family. But he was never about us kids or connected with us. That just wasn't his thing. So I didn't have a dad or a stepdad or really a man of any kind in my life while I was growing up."

The Void in a Daughter's Life

This book is not about fathers and daughters, about how crucial and important a caring, compassionate man is in a girl's life, especially as she navigates adolescence on the treacherous journey of becoming a woman. Yet we hear this theme repeated as we meet with women across North America and in other parts of the world. Time after time as we sit down with women who are busy coping with troubled marriages, we learn that while growing up, they didn't have sufficient attention or affection from their father or stepfather. We find that a deficit of male affection in those growing years often leads to struggle and difficulty in marriage. Today we hear yet another reminder of that recurring reality.

So by the time Sharon began dating and considering her future, she was coping with a serious deficit in compassionate, caring male attention. Small wonder that when Carl came along—a romantic, charming male—she immediately fell in love with him and wanted to get married. Her ability to discern and choose wisely had not been formed and shaped by a history of positive relationships with males.

The pattern is as old as time, and we find it all over the globe. It begins with a daddy deficit.

Several times in Sharon's narrative, she stops for a bit to regain her emotional composure. Although I'm not always a hugger by nature, I hug this new friend more than once. She receives my embraces eagerly, returning them with appreciation.

David brings us back to the question of the moment. "So when you met Carl, what was he like? For example, was he working then?

Did he seem to have a good income or a lot of money? Did he spend a lot of money on you or take you to nice places?"

Sharon thinks for a moment. "I didn't really pick up on things like that back then," she says. Now, as an older and wiser loan officer, she is more discerning as she investigates and considers potential customers' character and patterns.

"All I knew was that he was charming, he was in great shape physically, and he gave me a lot of compliments and kept telling me how pretty I was. I was seventeen; I hadn't realized yet that a man's character and his level of responsibility is so important later in life. All I knew was, here was this good-looking older guy who seemed to find me attractive. He kept paying attention to me, flattering me, wanting to be with me. He was relentless and wanted to be around me all the time.

"Looking back, I realize he wasn't spending much money on me. I didn't even notice because he was investing his time and attention in me and making me feel important. That was huge—I really hadn't gotten that before from a guy. But now that I look back, I realize that he wasn't spending much money on me.

"We didn't go out for dinner and a movie like some dating couples do. We usually went back to his house. He had two roommates, but they were never around. We'd order pizza and rent a movie, and that was kind of our big date night. Usually his roommates came home sometime during the evening, but they'd leave us alone."

She leans forward in her chair, making sure she has our full attention. "You just can't imagine how amazing that was. Just a simple thing like eating pizza with a guy and renting a movie and hanging out at his house…It made me feel older and more grown up. It made me feel like I was a person that someone would want to be with. It was exactly what I wanted at that time, and more. When I think about those days now, it seems like I was almost intoxicated by our relationship."

She pauses for a moment, so David asks another question. "How did your relationship turn into a marriage? Whose idea was that?"

Sharon pauses for a moment as a wry smile traces its way on her face. "Well, he asked me to move in with him," she admits. "And I was already spending most of my time over at his place anyway. I was only seventeen, but I had finished high school a year early, and I was still deciding whether I wanted to go to college. I liked being at his place a whole lot better than I liked being at home. At least at his place, somebody seemed to like me.

"One night he asked me to move in with him, and I almost said yes right then and there. Instead—and I don't even know why I did this—I told him I'd be glad to move in as soon as he bought me a ring. Two weeks later he surprised me with a ring, and that was that. I sort of became his third roommate, and the four of us shared that apartment for several months. We got married when I turned eighteen because I was old enough to sign for myself and didn't need my mom's permission."

Fire and Brimstone

Every once in a while as we travel, David and I will hear some rip-roaring, fire-breathing sermon about the evils of sex and how young people can get caught up in that trap to their own destruction. As we've gotten older, we have noticed that fairly often these same preachers eventually lose their ministries, often because of an issue related to sexuality. I am not sure what this means, but we've observed this pattern across several decades.

More than once we've listened to an angry, fiery sermon about the evils of homosexuality and then later discovered that the preacher was apparently struggling with his own same-sex issues. I do not say this to judge any of these preachers or question their motives.

From a woman's perspective, I'm not sure that sexual attraction is what drives a relationship to the kinds of arrangements people are making today. Was Sharon so sex-crazed at 18 that she rushed her way into an unwise marriage? Was she so addicted to the hormonal joys that flowed from the bedroom that she forgot to use wise judgment and get some sound, practical counsel from a minister or other adult? I don't think so.

What happened here, and what happens so very often, is this: A woman began her adult life with a serious deficit in male affection and attention. She lacked a model of healthy marriage and effective fathering. She grew up needing but lacking something, and as adulthood arrived and she gained a lot more freedom, she began looking for what was missing from her family background and her personal experience.

Sharon was not a sexual addict or a sexual predator as she came of age. She was just a typical teen girl from a dysfunctional family who suddenly experienced an emotional and relational rush when an older male noticed her. She was willing to trade sex (she moved in with Carl) for affection, attention, and the extra payoff of finally feeling like an adult. Not even knowing why, she bartered for a ring in the process, and she got it. Getting the ring wrapped a legal and socially approved bow around the primary gifts she was receiving in the transaction, which were affirmation and the appearance of respect.

In exchange for the use of her body in sexual encounters, she received things that greatly mattered to her, positive things she had never received. A male told her she was pretty, made her the center of his life and attention, and showered her with enough affection to keep her bonded to him and involved with him.

Can you understand why sexual temptation or addiction might not be the primary factor when a vulnerable young female makes this sort of arrangement? From her perspective, the transaction is not particularly about sex. It's about having a sense of permanence, family, and adulthood. It's about being told for the first time in her life that she is attractive and desirable. Sex is included in the mix, but it may not be the primary motivator.

I fear sometimes that we're preaching against the wrong things and missing out on the messages that we most need to be preaching.

I don't mean to defend Carl, but he may not have been on the prowl or seeking to devour a woman for his own selfish pleasure. He may have just noticed a pretty girl, hit on her a few times, and been surprised by his own success. He may have exploited and manipulated her, but he may also have simply followed his own hormones in a direction that turned out successfully from his point of view.

Life is less often a menacing plot and more often the juxtaposition of two needy people. In the barter system of a dating relationship, males often give away affection and attention because these things are relatively inexpensive and easy to improvise. Females often trade away the main assets they think they possess: their looks, their body, their sexuality. In return they receive attention, admiration, and affection—all of which they value and desire.

From such beginnings flow countless STDs, many unwanted pregnancies, and a steady stream of broken promises and shattered relationships. From such beginnings—when someone insists on and receives a marriage contract in the bargain—flow divorces, abandoned children, and a new generation of adults who come of age with their own attention and affection deficits, growing up in the ruins of a former family.

This is a vicious cycle needing the full attention of Christianity, but blaming it on our sex drives is shortsighted and may miss the mark. We humans are hardwired for relationships and meaning. We often derive our own sense of worth from the way others perceive us.

From a woman's perspective, and especially from an inexperienced woman's perspective, receiving a meaningful relationship may seem to be an acceptable tradeoff for sexual activity. It is this side of the equation, more so than sexual desire per se, that motivates so many young women into premature or unwise sexual involvement. In giving away sexual favors, an immature young woman may feel more fully valued, more like an adult, or more like someone who is desirable and respected.

It takes a very secure young woman to turn down a trade-off like that, and our culture is not raising nearly enough secure young women. Although teaching abstinence is valuable and worthwhile, we also need to be teaching self-respect, personal dignity, and the innate value of each one of God's children.

Faith Matters in the Dark Places

Sharon is secure and wise, mature and insightful. Eight years of marriage have formed and shaped her views about life and relationships. In addition, several years after marrying, she visited a Bible-believing church near her home and found her way to faith in Christ.

"I can't tell you how much finding Christ has meant to me," she tells us, starting to sound like an eager evangelist in a coffeehouse crowded with lost souls. "It has literally turned my life around. My faith has held me together in the tough times and kept me hoping for change when it didn't look like change was possible."

We ask about her church, and she gives us a glowing ten-minute description of a faith community where people can wear any kind of clothes to the services, say anything that's on their mind, and simply be who they are without needing to clean up their act or pretend to be perfect. There is even a designated smoking area outside in one corner of the parking lot.

"I never went to church growing up, so I didn't really have an idea of what it was, but this church is definitely not what I was expecting," our new friend tells us. "From the moment I walked in the front door I was surprised in a good way."

That initial surprise gave way to a faith encounter that has given Sharon hope for herself and for her marriage. But after eight years of dealing with an increasingly frustrating marriage, she wonders if it's time for some tough love or even if she needs to consider leaving her husband.

"He's changed so much," Sharon repeats. "Or maybe I just saw him through rose-colored glasses at first. All I know is, as soon as I got a steady job, he lost any interest in working. He hasn't really contributed financially to our household for a long time now. He drinks away his wages when he does work. We have a budget, but I made it and I keep us on it."

Six months after marrying, Sharon decided against college and applied for a part-time job as a bank teller. She discovered a natural affinity for finances, math, working with people, and helping others. Step-by-step her part-time role led to more responsibility. She became a full-time teller, then a trainer of new tellers, and then a supervisor of other tellers. Less than three years after being hired, she was training to be an assistant loan officer. Less than a year after that, in the quickest promotion the bank had ever granted, she became a loan officer.

"I enjoy my work so much," she tells us as a large family borrows the empty chair from our table. "I like helping people calculate what they ought to spend, how much they ought to borrow, how to stay within their budget. Right now I'm doing a lot of work helping people get out from under their credit card debt. It's sort of become my personal mission. I really feel like I'm helping people change their lives for the better and helping them move forward."

She pauses for a moment and then continues. "Ironically, my own life doesn't seem to be moving forward at all. I guess that's why I'm here."

"I've Never Talked to Anyone About This"

In eight years of increasing frustration, Sharon has never sought counsel from a minister, a friend, a sibling, or anyone else. All by herself, she's been coping with an unmotivated husband and a deteriorating marriage.

Carl hasn't left her, but he's completely checked out of the relationship. He isn't helping financially, he isn't doing any of the housework, he isn't pursuing her romantically, and he doesn't seem to be interested in sex. She's been making the house payment, making the car payment, fixing things when they break (Carl starts projects but doesn't finish them), and attending to a host of other household issues.

The experience has left her deeply bitter. "Sometimes I actually hate him. I look at him sitting there on the couch with his big beer belly and his sloppy jeans and his complete lack of personal grooming, and I find myself hating him. How did we grow so far apart?" she wonders aloud. "How did I start out loving this man and end up so frustrated and upset with him? Sometimes I can't stand to look at him. Just the sight of him makes me angry."

We're letting her vent for a while. After eight years, she's entitled. As we sit together in the busy coffee shop, she seems to be getting more relaxed as she talks about these things in a safe, nonjudgmental environment.

Can you imagine holding all this in for eight long years without complaining to any other person? If she's being candid with us, and she seems to be, this is exactly her condition. Eight years of suffering in silence. Eight years of increasing bitterness as her marriage relationship becomes less and less satisfying and her household arrangements become less and less fair and balanced. She loses her physical attraction to her husband, loses her respect for the man she married, and nearly (by her own admission) loses her own sanity.

We'd never recommend holding it in for eight years, but she's done a remarkable job of keeping herself together. We're impressed with her, and later in our session we'll tell her so. For now, we're listening to more of the bitterness as it pours out in streams, rich in detail and fully formed after years of incubation.

"I can't get him to bathe. The more I nag him about it, the longer he'll go without taking a shower or trying to clean up. Most of the time he actually smells bad. I sit there during the day at work, in my quiet office with my lovely plants and my nice desk, and I can almost smell him from right there. I dread going home because the place stinks! Isn't that terrible? And it stinks because Carl won't even get up off the couch and take a shower. Sometimes I cook spicy food just to overpower his smell, at least in the kitchen and the dining room."

Comments like these are spouting out of her now like steam from a boiling kettle, but at least now the kettle is not going to explode. Finally, the lid off has come off, and the pressure is released.

A High Achiever Despite the Odds

As we consider Sharon's anger and resentment, we are impressed that she's grown a lot since getting married at the very young age of

18. She has found Christ, found a job, and demonstrated responsibility, good character, and high aptitude. She has won a promotion, trained for a new role, obtained a higher-paying position, purchased a home, purchased a car, managed a household...and the list goes on.

We are meeting today with a 26-year-old woman who has accomplished much in a fairly short period of time. How many 26-year-olds have absolutely no student loans to pay off? How many have no credit card debt at all? How many have equity in their home and a late-model car in the driveway? How many achieve these things with only a high-school education and one income? In our view, Sharon is a success. She deserves our respect and admiration for all she's achieved. Even more remarkably, she's managed these things pretty much on her own, although she'd be quick to credit her faith in Christ and the help of a loving heavenly Father.

Yet while she was achieving these things and moving upward in maturity and financial accomplishment, Carl was in a downward spiral of no motivation, no employment, and frequently no bathing. To say these two were moving in opposite directions is somewhat of an understatement.

So for eight years, despite her own progress and success, Sharon has been building up more and more frustration, resentment, and internal anger toward a husband who once romanced her but now lies on the sofa switching channels all day.

"He watches Brazilian soap operas," Sharon tells us at one point. "I'm ready to send him down there so he can watch them in person."

Toxic Shock Syndrome

Unresolved bitterness is like that. It may begin slowly, starting out not as a major issue but as a collection of smaller frustrations that never seem to be addressed. The issues vary from wife to wife and from marriage to marriage, but they often sound like this:

"My husband is working too much. He doesn't spend enough time at home."

"My husband is spending too much money on his toys. He doesn't allocate enough of our income for food, doctor visits, and the other necessities."

"My husband wants sex when he wants it but not when I'm in the mood."

"My husband doesn't seem to want sex anymore. When I initiate it, he turns me away with some excuse about how busy he is."

"My husband doesn't help with the baby. Doesn't he notice how many disposable diapers we use around here?"

"My husband won't discipline the kids. He leaves it up to me to make sure their rooms are clean or they do their homework. He won't take any action, set any rules, or do any disciplining."

The issues vary, but the pattern is clear. A series of issues goes unaddressed, and before you know it, life seems unjust, and parts of the relationship seem unfair. And the longer an injustice prevails or the unfairness continues, the more freely bitterness and resentment creep into our hearts, taking up residence there and poisoning our minds and spirits. What begins as a series of small disappointments can easily escalate into toxic shock. Our souls are in danger.

Unresolved bitterness is a trap that ensnares many married women, both young and old. It's a pitfall we often don't see coming because we're focused on what we regard as the real problem. Our husbands won't help. Our husbands won't change. Our husbands aren't giving us enough attention. Our husbands are lazy or unmotivated or stubborn.

These issues may be valid and our perspective accurate. Sharon is not just imagining her difficulties. We wives can often accurately assess problems and clearly describe them, but we don't always realize how angry, bitter, and resentful we are becoming. Is it our fault that our husbands are underperforming? No. Are the issues imaginary? No. So in our sense of justice and self-righteousness, we often miss the many clues that our own emotional health is slipping. We miss what is right in front of us.

Within the confines of our own hearts, even if no one else can see it yet, our attitudes are starting to show. And our attitudes—just like Carl's bathing habits—can be downright stinky.

First Steps Toward Personal Health

Somewhere between the two extremes—leaving the bum and ignoring his problems—is the middle ground we seek with our new friend at Caribou. Although we don't rush toward a prescription, we do help her realize that over the course of eight long years, the daily injustice and unfairness in her life has caused a lot of bitterness, anger, and resentment to build up inside her.

That kind of buildup can destroy personal health and interpersonal relationships.

Regardless of whether Carl ever changes (more about outcomes in the last three chapters), what matters right now is that Sharon needs to change too. For the sake of her own health, she needs to work through the bitterness and anger and begin living life with a whole, undamaged heart.

These are choices she can make for herself. These choices do not depend on Carl's willingness to help, change, or leave. Sharon, on her own initiative and in her own time, can make much-needed improvement in her heart condition. As we sit with her in a St. Paul coffee shop, we begin gently pointing her in these directions, showing her the condition of her heart and the contours of change.

"You're right," she says after we've spoken to her for a while. "I've been holding on to so much anger. You can't even imagine." She leaves the thought unfinished, and we allow the silence to linger awhile. "I have become bitter. I have become resentful. When you talk about those things, I sit here and realize right now: That's who I am. That's what I've become after all these years of trying to deal with this. How did I end up this way? This isn't who I really am, deep down inside."

By God's grace, we've managed to go out for coffee before this woman goes into full-in cardiac arrest. She still has time to change her heart for the better.

At this point, you may be wondering, *Why are they picking on this poor woman? She's not the one to blame here! Why aren't they going after the husband for being a slob?*

Valid questions, but the answer is pretty simple. The slob isn't sitting with us in Caribou. We may never have the privilege of spending two hours with the slob—er, the husband. Meanwhile, the wife is directly in front of us. We're dealing with what we've been given.

Do you want us to counsel her to leave the bum? Sorry, we don't run around the globe dissolving marriages. We're pro-marriage by nature. Do you want us to counsel her to just ignore the problems? Sorry again. We don't believe that burying your head in the sand or continuing to endure the status quo are good choices. Ignoring problems doesn't make them go away.

We've been given a chance to sit down for two hours with a frustrated wife, a woman in whom anger, bitterness, and resentment have been boiling for the better part of eight long years. She's never told anyone. She has positive interaction with her coworkers, but she really doesn't have any close friends. So part of her silence is simply the absence of a network to confide in.

Health Happens

Two hours after we arrive, Sharon is visibly more relaxed and is taking a realistic look at her own reflection. She sees her own bitterness, anger, and resentment toward a husband who makes it hard to respect or even like him. With the guidance of two friendly counselors, this woman is taking ownership of her own heart condition and pledging with God's help to move forward to a healthier, more balanced perspective.

No one is beating up on Sharon or blaming her for being angry. Wouldn't you be angry if you walked in her shoes for eight years?

In our short time together, she has released a lot of resentment and has begun to install a new perspective. Even if her situation and circumstances never change, one thing is changing: her heart. She is releasing anger, releasing frustration, and resolving bitterness.

Use the questions below to review your own heart and life. Does unresolved bitterness have a place in your heart?

Reflections for Your Personal Journey

1. Think about the way Carl changed from the start of their relationship until the day of our Caribou appointment. What might be some reasons he let himself go after getting married? Is this typical of husbands in general, or is Carl an unusual case?

2. Think about your own husband's personal progress since you began dating, fell in love, and became engaged. Is he more attentive to you now or less attentive? Is he more mature now, more accomplished, more wise—or has he gone the other direction, seemingly becoming less mature and less responsible?

3. Do you and your husband have a workable plan for who accomplishes which chores and duties in your household? Did you reach that agreement after a mutual, positive discussion? Do you review your agreement from time to time to make sure it's still fair and balanced?

4. Right now, are you carrying responsibilities or duties that your husband should be handling instead? If so, make a list of these things.

5. Is your husband doing his share of the parenting? If you have a baby or infant in the house, does your husband deal with diapers or feedings? If you have older children, is he helping with homework or sharing some of your chauffeur duties, driving kids to soccer or other events?

6. Does your husband tend to be lazy or industrious? Would you like to see him become more relaxed or more motivated? Why?

7. Deep inside your heart, are you still angry or upset about something your husband once said or did? Are you frustrated by something that he does on a consistent basis? Do you

resent him for being unwilling to change even though you've told him what you expect and desire?

8. Does your husband make you feel attractive and desirable? Does he notice and appreciate your appearance, your fashion sense, or other aspects of your femininity? Does he build you up with his compliments, or does he tear you down with his words and his behavior?

9. Have you paid attention to the way your own heart responds to your husband's failings or frailties? Have you realized your tendency to store up a list of things you are frustrated or upset about?

10. If you were meeting Sharon at a coffee shop, and if you were hearing her story for the first time, what advice would you give her? What kind of outcome would you be hoping for in her marriage? What kind of outcome would you be hoping for in her heart?

11. Does Sharon remind you of yourself? How? Why? Do you struggle with unresolved bitterness? Are anger and resentment stored up in your heart?

Part 2

OUTCOMES:
When Changing Me Changes You

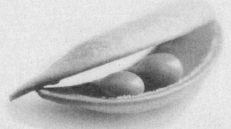

7

A Tale of Two Wives

Driving eastbound on the San Francisco–Oakland Bay Bridge, we're watching more than a dozen water-skiers chase brightly colored kites across the waves. It's the green way to parasail—no boat and no motor. Only the wind is powering these athletic dancers. They soar upward with their kites, ski swiftly across the waves, and occasionally wipe out in a burbling froth of foam.

It's an amusing adventure for me, but David keeps his grip on the wheel and his eyes on the road. We began our honeymoon right here, and although the Golden Gate Bridge draws all the attention, we like the San Francisco–Oakland Bay Bridge. Westbound, you cross into the heart of San Francisco, easily accessing most of the city's treasures. Eastbound is less scenic, but the bay itself is beautiful. Sailboats tilt against the wind at all angles.

Today we're en route to meet two wives whose stories we simply must hear while writing a book about becoming your husband's best friend. Since 1997 a large portion of our time has been consumed with writing several dozen articles and twelve books with four publishers. Some of our best stories have come to us as we finish speaking at a marriage event or a conference and someone catches us briefly in the hallway, interrupting us with a question or a comment or a referral.

"You need to talk with Jenny," a woman will tell me as I stand in line for a cup of coffee. "Her life is exactly what you're writing about in your book! Here, let me give you her e-mail address."

"I have a friend you should talk to," someone will say to David. "He's the marriage coordinator at his church, and I think he'd be a great source for your book. I'm pretty sure he's on LinkedIn. Here's how you spell his name…"

We make a sincere effort to follow up on every one of these unsolicited leads. Sometimes the trail grows cold or we never quite make the connection. Other times, we get incredibly lucky—or quite possibly we are led by divine, unseen hands that guide our journey toward higher outcomes than we could achieve on our own.

Signs of New Life

Our trail today leads to the new Emeryville Marketplace. Along the eastern edge of the San Francisco–Oakland Bay Bridge, a collection of dingy warehouses and nondescript office buildings has been supplanted by a bright array of condos, restaurants, and shops. It's an amazing transformation of a formerly forlorn neighborhood. Spreading out for blocks in all directions, new buildings form an urban community that is densely populated yet somehow feels like a village.

We rejoice in the path of progress. As we get closer to the area we can see a large theater anchoring one end of the development. Near it, the logo of a national bookstore chain thrusts prominently into the sky. We've been watching for that because we're meeting two wives in the second-floor coffee area of Barnes and Noble.

"It's huge," one of the wives had written in an e-mail, describing the gigantic new bookstore, which occupies two floors. "You won't have any trouble finding it."

"There it is!" I exclaim to my husband, who is busy searching for an inexpensive place to park our Honda. The women we are meeting have told us about a paid parking area nearby, but we're hoping to score a metered slot along one of the busy neighborhood streets. We've brought a pocketful of quarters, and we hope to buy parking in 15-minute bursts rather than paying for a full day or a large portion of it.

Okay, so we're cheap. In today's economy, we call that survival.

By divine grace or happy circumstance, a young couple is loading their Volvo wagon and is about to pull away from the curb. We watch them collapse an expensive imported stroller, herding two immaculately dressed children into the second seat of the car. The baby in the stroller is wearing a color-coordinated jumpsuit and hat, bundled against the Bay area's constant winds.

"There must be a Baby Gap hidden away in here somewhere," my husband wryly observes. This baby dresses better than we do. Perhaps he's a denizen of nearby Marin County, one of the most upscale zip codes along the California coast.

We watch as the non-fussy baby is snapped into her place in the car seat. The husband stows half a dozen shopping bags in back as the wife gives us a friendly wave. "We're leaving," she calls out to me with a bright smile. With respect to our friends in Boston and Bangor, the West Coast is definitely the friendlier one.

"Thank you," is the most creative response I can come up with. I smile at her, and in just moments we're angling our minivan into the wagon's former slot here on the main street of the development. It's our lucky day: There are a full 38 minutes left on the parking meter.

Happily walking hand in hand, David and I pass a shop that apparently sells only cupcakes. Can people make a living with such a one-dimensional offering? How do they pay a Bay-area mortgage on the strength of a few small round baked goods? How many people detour out of their way, pay to park, and rush in to buy cupcakes?

We're a few minutes early for our appointment, so we venture into the store to find out. We're not really intending to purchase anything here because we expect to buy coffee and scones for a party of four a few minutes from now in the bookstore. Our brief detour into cupcake land is strictly for information gathering, not for dining or purchasing. We're just looking, and perhaps also we'd like to inhale the aroma of chocolate or powdered sugar.

Three employees in matching aprons watch us walk through the door.

"Would you like a sample?" asks a girl who is perhaps 15 or 16 years old. "We're sampling our Red Velvet cupcakes today."

At least it's not Lent, and I haven't given up Red Velvet.

Moments later David and I are noshing on Red Velvet cupcake samples. Today a sample is a half-cupcake. The frosting is buttery smooth; the cake filling is moist to perfection. I have never tasted such an exquisite cupcake. Now I understand how this store survives.

"We, uh…maybe we should pick up a few of these for the trip home," David says. Out of respect for his culinary opinion, I agree. We leave the store with the samples added to our waistlines and a carry-out pack of four cupcakes added to the portfolio and purse we were already toting. Forgive us, but we don't offer the cupcakes to the two women we are about to meet.

Wandering Eyes

Meeting in a bookstore is easy. We walk in the door, immediately noticing the escalators to the second floor. While we are riding upward, the two women call out to us from somewhere above us. "We could see you walking over here," Heather and Lori exclaim while waving at us over the wooden railing of the second floor. "We totally knew that was you two from your picture on the website!"

Moments later we are seated at a small table near the coffee counter. Customer seating is very limited here, and we've considered taking our coffee and scones outdoors. But it's a windy day, and the inside seating seems better for conversation, counseling, and storytelling.

"You should go first," Heather tells Lori. "Your story is a lot more interesting than mine."

By now we've exchanged brief introductions. The two women have shown a high level of interest in this manuscript. Both of them tell us they've seen amazing transformations in their husbands. Both of them assure us that the changes in their husbands were precipitated not by direct action or insistent request, but instead as a consequence of the wives changing their own hearts, their own attitudes, and their own behavior patterns. As we listen attentively and ask reflective questions, we realize that their stories are perfect for this book.

"It's a good thing I had three girlfriends," Heather begins. She is smiling at us, but the intensity in her eyes shows us she's serious about this opening statement. "The first two gave me really unhelpful advice. If it hadn't been for Lori (the third girlfriend), I probably wouldn't be in my marriage today. And there's no way my marriage would be the amazing gift of God that it's become if I hadn't had her to go to for advice and wisdom."

"All I did was tell you my own story," Lori reminds her friend quietly. "I didn't try to give you advice, I just told you what God had done for me. From there, you made your own decision."

Heather smiles. "All I know is, without your advice I'd be divorced, raising my kids alone, and my husband would never have become the man he is today. My first two girlfriends weren't sending me in helpful directions."

Married for almost six years, Heather is a mother of two and the wife of a man with what she calls wandering eyes.

"I had gained about fifteen pounds after my first baby," Heather tells us. "And then after Serena was born, I gained another ten or fifteen pounds. So I was about twenty-five or thirty pounds heavier than I was when we got married, but I didn't usually feel fat. I was abnormally thin in college, and I kind of filled out after I got married. I started cooking at home, we began to have kids…and I put on some weight."

Heather's husband, always outgoing and flirtatious by nature, began cultivating relationships with other females, from older teens to nearly middle-aged women. The key was attractiveness. If an attractive female was anywhere near him, Heather's husband would notice her, pay attention to her, and begin a flirtatious conversation if he could.

"It could happen anywhere," Heather recalls as we sip our coffees. "Even in church. We would be picking up our kids at the nursery or dropping them off for child care, and James would be flirting with the other moms who were skinny, or blonde, or attractive. He'd have them laughing in no time, and if they turned out to be a good audience, he'd talk to them for ten minutes or more for no reason at all."

The visual issues were everywhere in Heather's world.

"He could somehow scope out an attractive female wherever she was, and his eyes would follow her forever. We'd be riding in the car together, and if we saw some attractive girl in shorts or on a bicycle, he'd just be glued to her for as long as she was in our sight. I remember thinking we were going to have a wreck someday because he'd be looking at some skimpily dressed blonde instead of watching the road.

"And don't even get me started about his TV viewing," Heather continues. "He'd watch any show that had girls in swimsuits, girls in shorts, girls getting slimed in the mud or knocked off a raft or whatever. The key was attractive girls—if you put them on television, my husband would find the show and watch it."

Never the most self-confident of women, Heather became depressed and disappointed. "Maybe if he'd been giving me that same kind of attention, I wouldn't have minded so much that he shared it with others. But he was focusing his attention on everyone else and ignoring me. He never took the time to make me feel attractive or desirable or wanted."

Heather tried to keep her focus on raising her two young children, but her heart longed for a husband who found her attractive. "I'd buy cute outfits or get my hair done," Heather remembers, "but nothing I did seemed to matter. He could flirt with anybody at Walmart or at church—even the younger moms in our neighborhood—but it seemed like he didn't even see me."

Really Bad Advice

Heather turned to her closest friends for support.

"The first girlfriend I talked to was on her second marriage, but it was going good at the time. She told me I should have an affair! She was totally serious. She told me the only way I could break through my husband's fog was to let him think he was losing me to somebody else. She told me to go out and start an affair and then confess it to my husband so he would know there was another guy.

"She actually told me that if I wanted him back, that was the only way to get his attention," Heather tells us. "And even though there is no way I'd ever do that, I did find myself kind of thinking about it after she said that. I found myself dreaming about flirting with some other guy and him flirting back and then maybe my husband catching us flirting.

"I just wanted my husband to see some other guy finding me attractive," Heather admits. "I never actually considered having an affair, but I started to daydream about flirting with guys on purpose, just to get caught. I had two little kids at home, and there was no way I would start an affair or cheat on my husband. I'll admit I was fantasizing about it in unhelpful ways, but my silly daydreams were never going to turn into reality. It was probably the most stupid advice I've ever gotten from anybody!"

The three of us are inclined to agree as we listen to this part of Heather's story. An affair as the cure for a husband's lustful eyes? Yes, that definitely qualifies as stupid advice. And Heather's second girlfriend was not helpful either, although her idea initially made much more sense.

"My second girlfriend told me to file for a divorce," Heather recalls. "She didn't start by saying that, but that's what it came down to. Every time I saw her, she just kept telling me that I deserved to be with someone who appreciated me.

"She didn't know it, but those comments really hit me hard. I mean, she kept saying that I deserved to be respected, that I deserved to be appreciated, that I was a beautiful person, and that I deserved to be with a man who knew that.

"Every time she said that, something inside of me would agree with her. When my first girlfriend would tell me to cheat on my husband, nothing in me would agree to that. But when my second girlfriend started telling me I deserved better—my whole heart said yes, I do deserve better. Yes, I do deserve to be respected by a man!

"I didn't want a divorce because it's messy and it screws up the kids," Heather tells us in frank language. "But I thought maybe if I filed for a divorce, that would get my husband's attention so much that he would start to change. I thought I wouldn't have to actually go through with a divorce, I just needed to start one."

Complicating matters was a series of billboards that went up in Heather's community at the time. "Everywhere I drove right then," Heather says, "I kept seeing these billboards advertising easy divorces for just $99. They had a toll-free number that I actually wrote down a couple of times but never called. I couldn't believe that filing for a divorce could be so cheap! I started thinking about saving back some grocery money, getting the $99 together, and filing."

Heather shakes her head in disbelief. "Sometimes, I was really close to doing that. I thought that $99 would change my life for the better, and I'd be a fool if I didn't spend the money and file the papers."

Breakfast and a Breakthrough

Happily for Heather, her children, and her marriage, she had more than two girlfriends. Lori was about to change Heather's life forever just by being there.

"I was at Chick-fil-A one morning," Heather continues, "and I noticed this woman from church. I knew her name was Lori, so that morning I just said hello. I was taking my kids to breakfast because they love Chick-fil-A and our local restaurant is always having kids' promotions.

"Anyway, that morning I just walked over and said hello. My kids were old enough to play quietly by themselves for a bit. Lori was a great listener, and I ended up telling her things that I really hadn't told anyone before—not either of my two girlfriends or even my mom. So we are sitting there in a busy Chick-fil-A with my kids playing nearby, mostly coloring on their placemats, and I'm crying and Lori is crying and both of us probably look completely crazy. But it was so what I needed right then. It was like God woke Lori up, told her she better get to Chick-fil-A, and she obeyed right away."

"God did put us together that day," Lori adds, "but I'm not sure it was such a miracle. I eat at Chick-fil-A two or three mornings a week. So that day was not really any different for me. I work part-time, starting at ten in the morning, so I like to stop off at Chick-fil-A around nine, after most of the breakfast crowd has gone, and just read my paper, have some breakfast, and start my day."

Heather laughs. "Okay, so maybe it wasn't a miracle you were there. But it was a miracle that you listened to me and understood me and helped me. And what God has done in my marriage since then has definitely been a miracle."

Lori agrees. "Yeah, your marriage has been a miracle since then."

"Anyway," Heather continues as she turns back to us, "Lori told me her own story, which you'll hear in a minute. And I couldn't believe how similar it was to what I was feeling and what I was going through. Then when she told me how God had worked in her own heart first and how God had given her husband such a complete makeover, I just sat there in shock.

"I was crying when I listened to Lori's story just because I couldn't believe how good God was being. Even in my daydreams I wasn't quite able to imagine my husband being loving and caring and attentive. I just wanted him to stop being so psychologically involved with everyone else! I couldn't really imagine him getting tunnel vision all of a sudden and really focusing on just me.

"But the more I listened to Lori's story, the more I knew it was possible. I couldn't get away from her testimony about what God had done in her own heart. I couldn't quit listening to how God had changed her husband and his attitudes. The more I listened, the more I realized this was the first good advice anyone had given me. I'm so glad I wanted a chicken biscuit that morning!"

Redirecting the Focus 180 Degrees

"Basically, what Lori told me was to change my focus," Heather continues. "She told me I was sitting there all the time wanting my husband's attention—which I was. And she said instead of doing that, I should focus on giving my attention to my husband, making him feel desirable and attractive and valued.

"It sounds easy to say, but it was a complete shift of what I was feeling and thinking and worrying about. I had never once stopped to think about how James felt when he walked in the front door of our townhouse. I had been so caught up in feeling neglected, feeling like he didn't appreciate me, feeling like he didn't even see me. I never once stopped to think about how he felt."

Lori's wise counsel sparked a complete paradigm shift in Heather. Heather was still dealing with the same situation, but now she saw it from a fresh perspective. Her own needs became secondary. Her focus shifted to helping to meet her husband's needs—even if he didn't deserve the respect she was about to provide.

"James was still being a jerk!" Heather says with bright laughter and without any apparent bitterness. "It wasn't like he changed that same day or anything. I was the one who changed that day. I went home from Chick-fil-A as a different person, ready to focus on different things. My mind-set was completely changed.

"Before I left the restaurant that morning, I asked Lori to pray for me. She wrapped one arm around my shoulder and started praying out loud. I bet everyone was freaked out to see these two women praying together and crying. But at that moment I was so desperate, I really didn't care.

"If God could change my marriage the way He had changed Lori's, I wanted in. I wanted the same kind of changes for our home and our kids. I wanted to see God work in powerful ways. I was ready to let Him start with me, not with somebody else. After I listened to Lori tell me her story, I wanted God to start changing my story. I was ready to do whatever I needed to do so God could work."

Husbands of Happy Wives

Heather doesn't know it at the time, but she's in the midst of telling us exactly the kind of story that we're collecting for this book. We're looking for wives who have had close encounters with God that changed them forever. And we're finding that often, when a wife is changed in such a radical way, her husband and her marriage begin to change too.

Husbands resist nagging, begging, whining, and pleading. They rarely yield to straight-on approaches or confrontation. But somehow as a difficult husband begins to live with a newly humble and freshly inspired wife, God's grace is released in new places and in new ways. We can chart this change in marriage after marriage around the world.

Heather is practically preaching to us now. "My husband didn't change at that time. I changed," she says again. "I went home determined to focus on making my home a happy, healthy, attractive, inviting place—a place my husband would want to be. I went home determined to be someone my husband would want to spend more time with.

"I've been told some pretty weird things in my life, even at church. I've been told that a good wife should dress up in sexy clothes—or no clothes at all—or do all kinds of things in order to attract her husband and catch his attention. This wasn't anything like that. This was about me becoming focused on helping, serving, greeting, and smiling.

"I didn't realize how long I'd been resenting James for ignoring me and flirting with everyone else in a skirt. Once I released all of that resentment, I was able to focus on being a great mom to my kids, getting in the best shape of my life—for me, not for a man—and making my home a happy, healthy, inviting place to be.

"The difference was tangible. My kids noticed how happy I was. One day my oldest asked me why I was so happy now. I almost cried! Even she could see the difference in me, and she was only five years old."

We ask Heather when she sensed the change beginning to happen in her husband's heart.

"There wasn't really one moment," Heather says, thinking about our question. "There wasn't a supernatural event or anything like that. But about three weeks after I started being a whole new person, we were finishing our dinner, and I started picking up after the kids. And right in the middle of that—I mean, it wasn't a sexy moment or anything, and I was definitely not wearing any sexy clothes—my husband suddenly said, 'You look really nice today.'"

"I almost fell on the floor. I was facing away from him, grabbing a broom out of the pantry, and I was so glad he couldn't see my face. I was in shock! When I sort of regained my composure, I turned around and said thanks and just smiled at him. I didn't say anything stupid back to him, like 'Wow, why haven't you said that in the past three years?' I just smiled and said thanks."

Heather pauses and smiles, enjoying the memory.

"About three weeks after that, he came home from work one day and asked me if I needed any help around the house. I don't know how I kept my face calm and natural because I was in complete shock all over again. He had never helped much around the house. In fact, I think this was the first time I could remember him offering.

"It caught me so off guard, and I was so unprepared…I wasn't smart enough or fast enough to even think of something he could do. He had never asked before! So I just smiled and told him I thought everything was under control. And then I smiled at him again and said thanks.

"Later that week he started finding stuff to do around the house and ways to help out. He picked up the stuff in our son's room, which is always a mess. He cleared the dishes one night after we ate pizza in the living room. Just little things…but believe me, he had never offered to do anything like that in our whole marriage.

"So no, I can't point to a moment, but I can sure tell you some of the first things that happened as the change began. He just started being nicer to me, and not just because he wanted sex."

Speaking of Sex…

Heather smiles again. "But speaking of that, he started wanting me again. It had been a while since anything like that was happening in our lives!" Heather chuckles at the memory. "He started coming after me with his hands again, just like he did when we were dating," she says with a laugh, and we all join in.

For all of the complaints we get from husbands about their wives not being interested in sex or not being involved when they have sex, we hear just as many complaints from wives that their men have seemingly lost interest. Heather's anecdote about her husband suddenly returning to interest in sex is indicative of a larger shift in her husband's attitude and behavior. Although he probably didn't know it himself, Heather's husband was finding his wife more attractive as a person—her attitude, her demeanor, her words, her behavior, her smile—and these intangible but very real changes in Heather were changing the way her husband saw her.

Eventually, Heather did lose some weight—for her own sake. She didn't do it to win back her man or to become anyone's sex kitten. She got herself in great shape because she understood it was a healthy and wise choice for her to make. Of course, it was also a good example for her children and a benefit for her husband as well. Heather dropped all of her post-pregnancy pounds and then kept going, joining a Christian kickboxing group and sharing in regular exercise sessions with women from her church. Today, Heather says she's in the best shape of her entire adult life. She's several sizes smaller than she was at her wedding.

"But James didn't start paying attention to me because I was skinny," Heather insists. "My weight loss came later. James totally changed the way he treated me even while I was still carrying my extra weight. It wasn't like I suddenly started parading around the house wearing bikinis and looking like a supermodel, so then he paid attention to me! I was still exactly the same as before, the real me, and I had a few extra pounds here and there. But even at that time, James started being interested in sex again. He started helping me put the kids to bed a little bit early so we could go to bed a little bit early too."

"Today," Heather continues after a brief pause, "we have a pretty good marriage. I'm not ready to call it a 'great' marriage yet. I'm not even sure I know what a great marriage looks like. But we have a pretty good marriage. We don't fight very often, we get along pretty good, and I know my husband likes me and finds me attractive. And I feel good about myself."

Let It Begin with Me

Lori jumps in at this point. "I'm not trying to start my story already, but it's very similar at that point. I changed me—for me—and felt good about that by itself. Later there were some amazing changes in Bob, but that isn't how it started."

"Exactly," Heather agrees. "When I became a more positive, loving, and unselfish person, my whole life began to feel better. James hadn't changed at all yet—he was still behaving like a jerk. But once I started being positive and supportive and loving and unselfish, it was like I was living in a whole different world while still in the same place."

Lori smiles. "That's what I tried to tell Heather way back then when we both started crying. That's why I think our stories are so powerful. We just tell people about what God did in us, and it's after that when the changes started happening in other people, including our husbands. Looking back, I realize how immature I was. I was focused on how my husband was messing up our marriage and our future. All I could think about was his mistakes, his bad behavior, his being selfish and unreasonable, so I couldn't see my own faults and flaws. Once I got a look at me, I knew I needed to change regardless of what happened in my marriage or my family. I needed to change because it was time for me to grow up and start being the woman and the person that God created me to be."

Lori has started to tell us about a life changed by God, and we're eager for more of the details. Heather makes the transition.

"That's pretty much what I wanted to say," Heather concludes. "I mean, I'd love to recruit every woman in the world into my kick-boxing class, but exercise and working out and getting in shape aren't really the point of my story. The point is that I realized I was out of shape spiritually, and I decided to let God work on my heart and my mind and my attitudes. I hadn't realized I was so spiritually immature. That's where God started working on me. He's not done yet—I still have a lot of growing up to do. But today when I look in the mirror, I can see where God has already brought a lot of good changes into my attitudes and my actions."

Real Life, New Life

Lori affirms her friend's claim. "Heather is a brand-new person today, compared to when I met her," Lori asserts. "You can see it in her face. I'm not talking about wearing makeup or losing pounds or keeping the house clean. I'm talking about the glow that you see when you are talking to a godly woman, and you just sense the Spirit of God in her whole presence. Before, she was so stressed out, so emotionally tired, so physically at the end of herself. She had a lot of questions spiritually, like we all do. I mean, all of us who end up in bad marriages ask why God lets that happen and why He doesn't step in and change our husbands. All of us pray, and then maybe we don't see any answers, or at least not any quick ones, and we get discouraged.

"So we have our questions and our issues. We deal with depression and frustration. And we begin to wear that around even on our faces. I wish I had a video of Heather talking then so you could compare it with the way she talks today. You'd see what I mean. You'd see the changes on her face, in the tone of her voice…even in the way she sits and stands. She is literally a whole new person, and I don't mean a smaller jeans size or dress size. I mean that today she has a spiritual energy and a personal joy that she didn't have when we first talked together."

Heather is nodding her head this whole time, agreeing with her friend. "Back then, I didn't see it in myself. But when I met Lori, one of the things that really affected me was her positive energy—the joy of the Lord that just flowed out of her. She sat there telling me the most horrible things about her own life and her own marriage, but she said those things while almost glowing with positive energy.

"She was praising God even while talking about the rough places and the darker moments of her journey. That really impacted me. I mean, I don't get very blessed when someone praises God without experiencing what I call real life. Someone who hasn't been through all the hassles and the difficulty and the suffering...when they praise God, I guess that's okay, but it doesn't connect with me.

"But Lori was talking about real stuff, some of it horrible, and while she did that, she was praising God and thanking Him for His goodness to her. That made me sit up and listen. That made me really pay attention. It made me want what she had found," Heather tells us. "And I was restless after talking to Lori that first time. I wanted to be on the journey that she was on, and I wanted to start immediately. God showed up, and with His help I began to change, right then and there."

Heather smiles at Lori; the two of them appear to be near tears.

First Things First

It's time for us to hear Lori's story, and after Heather's powerful testimony we're ready to listen! But Lori seems to minimize or downplay her own role in the situation. She is humble and genuine, not showy or overdramatic.

"Can we pray before I begin?" Lori asks us. "I always like to pray before I tell anyone my story because I want to get it right. I don't want people thinking I did some big thing or I'm somebody special. I was just a wife in a very hard place, and God met me there, right where I was, and started helping me to be different. So my story is about God, not about me."

We agree to let Lori pray, and she does. Her prayer is simple and sincere, not filled up with big words or flowery phrases. She doesn't quote Scripture in her prayer or even sound very spiritual. Instead, she sounds as if she is talking to a friend. Her prayer seems like a natural part of our conversation.

When Lori finishes praying, all of us feel better. The tone in the room has changed, and all of us feel it.

"Thank you for praying," David tells her. "I think all of us were aware of God's presence while you were praying. What a great way to begin your story."

Ignoring the Danger Signals

"I was married to Heather's husband," Lori says with a smile. "Not literally, but I mean a man much like him. That's one reason Heather and I connected so quickly. Both of us married the same type of person.

"When Bob and I were dating, he was the biggest flirt in the world. But that didn't bother me because he wasn't going out with all those other girls, he was going out with me! In a strange way, that made me proud. I was like, here is this popular guy who flirts with every-body, and they all flirt right back at him, but he doesn't want any of them. He wants me! It really boosted my self-esteem. So instead of bothering me it made me feel good back then. Now I realize that I was prideful. I had never been super confident, especially not about the way I looked. So to have this popular, flirty guy make me the center of his attention—wow, that was an ego boost and a confi-dence builder.

"But Bob was showing his true colors even before we got mar-ried," she tells us slowly. "I wasn't seeing any of the red flags because I was too busy enjoying being confident and desirable. I missed all the danger signs because I was caught up in my own pride.

"I don't know why I thought everything would change when we got married, but I actually did," Lori admits. "I mean, marriage is different than dating, you know? When you marry someone, you narrow your choices. You quit playing the field, and you agree to be with just one person, not a whole bunch of people.

"That's what marriage is. So when Bob proposed to me, and I imme-diately said yes, I just assumed he would focus on me when I was his wife. I thought we both had the same idea of what marriage was."

David interrupts briefly. "Premarital counseling is supposed to focus on issues exactly like that. What do you think marriage will be like? What does your partner think marriage will be like? In premarital counseling, you work on all of that and talk about all of that—you get it out in the open."

Heather and Lori are nodding their heads in agreement.

"Well, we didn't have much of that," Lori confesses. "We got married in my church, and my pastor had known me my whole life, and he just kind of skipped ahead to the ceremony. We didn't really have any of those conversations where you talk about what you're expecting from marriage."

David nods. "I didn't mean to interrupt your story. It's just that I get a little bit preachy on the subject of counseling before marriage or remarriage." David smiles, and the rest of us do too.

"I wish we'd had some," Lori says.

Changes Fast and Furious

"Anyway, Bob and I got married, and I was pregnant almost immediately. We didn't take a honeymoon, but obviously we had sex a lot in that first month or two, and I got pregnant right away. I wasn't planning on that. Neither of us were, but there it was. It just happened to us. So I am a brand-new bride, and before you know it I start getting fat and hating the way I look.

"I mean, isn't it supposed to be exciting when you're pregnant? Aren't you supposed to be flooded with the joy of new life or something?" Lori looks around at all us, wondering about this.

"When I'm pregnant, I just feel fat," Heather says, laughing.

"Well, that's how I felt too," Lori agrees. "There I was, a brand-new bride, never married before, and I'm out shopping for maternity clothes because I don't fit into my jeans, and I don't like the way I look.

"Meanwhile, Bob is flirting with everyone. He flirts with my girlfriends. He flirts with the women at church, old and young. He flirts with our next-door neighbors, who are three single girls sharing a house. He flirts with everybody! And the more he flirts, the more I get mad at him. I mean, he's the reason I'm fat all of a sudden! He's the reason I look all bloated while the three girls next door just look hot."

Heather nods in complete agreement, and Lori continues. "So I'm in my first few months of being married, and I'm getting fat, and Bob is flirting with everything that breathes, and I'm just getting more and more angry with him. Needless to say, my anger didn't help our relationship any. A lot of the time he couldn't figure out why I was so mad at him. And my hormones were fluctuating anyway, so sometimes I felt like a complete basket case, and one thing just led to another."

Fighting and Fooling Around

"We started fighting all the time. You know, about the only thing that was still working was our sex life. Even while I got fat, he was wanting me sexually. But then he'd go out the next day and spend two hours flirting with the neighbor girls, offering to help with lawn work or car care or whatever they needed. He'd be over there drinking a cold beer while I was at home getting fatter by the minute."

Lori stops her story long enough to look around the coffee shop. "We still had a good sex life until very late in my pregnancy," she tells us quietly. "But apart from that, all we did was fight."

Bob and Lori went on to have three children in the first five years of their marriage even though their relationship had deteriorated to mostly just fighting and sex. "We had makeup sex a lot," Lori says with a wry wrinkle on her face. "Looking back, most of our sex was makeup sex. We'd get all upset and start fighting, and somehow it would end up with us having sex.

"I was a mother of three before I was 26 years old. I was married to a guy who flirted with everyone else while I stayed home raising three little kids that we hadn't really planned for. Back when we were dating, both of us talked about having kids later, maybe after we'd been married for three or four years. What happened to that? Why didn't we stick with that for a plan?"

Lori sighs. "Looking back at those years, I can see how I turned into a whole different person," she admits. "I spent most of my first years of marriage feeling fat and being angry. I felt trapped and blamed my husband. I yelled at my kids and at him. I hated my life, to tell you the truth. I didn't hate my kids, but I hated the fact that I had kids—do you see the difference? I was a pretty good mom except for being angry all the time, but I was a lousy wife.

"I don't mean to make excuses for Bob's flirting, but I'm still learning to take responsibility for my own mistakes because I made a lot of them as a young married woman. I messed up a lot of things. I was an angry, yelling, upset wife and a grumpy mom to my kids. Maybe that's why I missed all the signals."

The Truth Comes Out

But then, everything changed. About seven years into her marriage, while Lori was the mother of three and while Lori and Bob were still fighting frequently, Lori ran across an e-mail message that he had printed out.

"I wasn't snooping," Lori tells us. "It's not like I was accessing Bob's e-mail account and reading through his messages, looking for anything. I knew he was a big flirt, and I spent a lot of time being mad at him, but I wasn't suspicious of anything, and I wasn't snooping around on his computer.

"But I saw an e-mail message that he had received and printed out. I didn't recognize the sender's name because it was a screen name, like Hot4U82 or something like that. I couldn't believe what I was reading. The sender was talking about all the things they did together—sexual things, and she was very explicit—and telling him she wanted to do those things again soon. I sat there in shock. I couldn't believe it was really happening. I thought maybe it was a made-up thing or a fantasy world or…I don't know what I thought. I didn't want to see it for what it was—evidence that my husband had been having sex with someone else for quite a while.

"I read that message about 20 or 30 times in a row, and still I didn't get it. My eyes kind of glazed over, and I felt like a big weight had dropped right on top of me. I couldn't move. I could hardly breathe."

That night, after putting the kids to bed, Lori dropped the bomb. "Hey, who is Hot4U82?"

"Oh, that's Jackie next door," Bob said with a laugh. "That's her screen name. She's the biggest flirt in the world. I think she's crazy!" Bob acted as if it was no big deal.

Lori pulled out the e-mail message that Bob must have enjoyed reading so much that he decided to print it out. She handed it to Bob, who read about three words and knew exactly what he was looking at.

"Uh," Bob mumbled, "I need to get something at the store." Before they could have a conversation, he was out the door, in his car, and driving away.

Denial

Lori is telling us these things in her quietest voice. She is very matter-of-fact, not overly dramatic or speaking with emotion.

"He didn't deny anything, he just got up and left," Lori remembers. "I waited for him for a while, but then I finally went to bed.

"He came home very late that night and crawled into bed. I woke up but pretended to be asleep. I didn't want to deal with it either, and I really didn't know where to start. I was just glad he came home."

The next morning Bob left for work as if everything were normal. Lori waited two weeks to confront Bob again.

"Alright, okay…I mean, you can read it for yourself!" Bob finally told her. "I guess you can see what's been going on. What do you want me to say?"

Lori sighs as she tells us these things. "I don't know how he did it, and I don't remember our exact conversation, but as we talked, Bob was making *me* feel guilty for reading his private e-mail message. He wasn't taking any responsibility at all for cheating on me. He wasn't dealing with that at all."

Lori remembers wanting to grab her kids, head out the door, get a divorce, and never look back. "I had been so angry for my whole married life, and suddenly for the first time I had a very legitimate reason to be angry. But for some reason, I didn't have any anger left in me. I just wanted to quit. I wanted to give up, end the marriage, leave town, take my kids, and start over.

"It wasn't like I even wanted control over my kids at that point. I just didn't want them to grow up with a flirt and a cheater for a dad. I didn't see how that could work. All I thought about was taking the kids and going away somewhere. Anywhere. It really didn't matter."

A Cry for Help

Lori is very quiet as she continues. "I don't know why I didn't do that. Maybe God stopped me. All I know is that one afternoon while Bob was at work and the kids were outdoors and my youngest one was sleeping, I just kind of cried out to God for help. I just kind of asked God to take everything and make it better.

"I didn't hear God's voice or anything, but I felt like I should open up my Bible and read. So I looked around the house, found my Bible, and started reading the first chapter of First John. It seemed like every word I was reading spoke exactly to my heart. The more I read, the more I knew that I needed to confess to God and get right with Him. I wasn't exactly in a place to argue about that. I knew I needed help."

Lori pauses, takes a long sip of ice water, and looks at us. "Reading my Bible that day, I didn't think about how much Bob needed to confess or how Bob needed to get right with God. I just thought about me, about how angry I'd been and about all the fighting in our house. I was ready to let God change my life, so I told Him so. And right there in that moment, in my dining room all by myself, I just gave God control of my life. I just told Him how sorry I was for everything, and asked Him to forgive me. I wasn't talking to Him about my husband or about the affair or anything like that. I just talked to God about me, and what I needed."

Forgive Me?

Lori, David, and I are silent.

"When Bob came home that night, he could tell I was different," Lori recalls. "He looked at me during dinner, with the kids right there, and asked, 'Are you leaving me or something?' The kids didn't really hear him or didn't realize what he meant. But Bob could see that something had changed in me. He just didn't know what.

"I asked him if we could talk about it after the kids went to sleep," Lori remembers, "and he said yes."

That night, with the children safely tucked away in bed, Lori told Bob about that day's encounter with God. "I apologized to Bob that night," she tells us. "I mean, I think it's very obvious how much Bob needed to apologize to me, and that hadn't happened. But that night I didn't talk about his affair or ask him for details. I just kept my focus on apologizing to him.

"I told him how sorry I was about yelling at him. I apologized for being angry for most of our married lives. I told him that I didn't know if our future was together or apart, but mostly I just needed him to know I was sorry for the way I had behaved as a wife.

"At one point in that conversation—and I was crying pretty much the whole time—I told Bob that he deserved better than what he had gotten. I told him that he deserved a wife who was positive and supportive and encouraging. I told him I was so sorry for how angry I had been. I asked him to forgive me.

"I told him I had no idea what was going to happen to us, but I just needed him to forgive me for how I had been. I kept asking him, 'Can you forgive me? Will you forgive me?'"

As she tells us this part of her story, Lori is crying softly. Heather is crying softly. I am crying softly. David has moisture at the edges of his eyes too.

"I wasn't excusing his behavior," Lori tells us between sniffles. "I wasn't forgiving his behavior, and he wasn't asking for forgiveness. All I did was talk about the things I had done wrong in our marriage, and there was plenty to talk about. I kept my focus on that, and I kept telling him how sorry I was."

At that moment, caught up in an emotional conversation, Bob

wasn't ready to forgive his wife. Whatever he was thinking or feeling, he kept to himself.

"This isn't your fault," Bob kept telling Lori that night. "This has nothing to do with you at all."

But Lori persisted, telling Bob she was sorry and asking for his forgiveness.

One Day at a Time

Three weeks later, Bob and Lori were still living in the same house, still married. Lori, by her own account, had become a completely new person. She got up in the morning, read a few words in a daily devotional book, and tried to focus on being a positive, happy, well-adjusted mom and wife. She put upbeat praise music on her iPod and listened to it for most of the day.

"At that point, I wasn't trying to solve our problems or save our marriage," Lori tells us. "I wasn't sure our marriage had a future. I wasn't making any plans. Looking back, I'm pretty sure I wouldn't have stayed with him if he was going to keep having sex with our neighbor," she says dryly. "But right then, I wasn't trying to solve all that. It took all my energy just to be positive, to let God make me a new person, and to be helpful to my kids and happy around the house. That was as much as I could focus on. When I tried to think about the future or our marriage, it was just too overwhelming.

"You know that old song called 'One Day at a Time'? That song kept going through my head. I just thought to myself that I needed to get through one day. Then the next day. I didn't have any other plan. I just had one purpose: to become a new kind of person with God's help."

About three weeks after that, Bob told Lori that they needed to talk. After the kids were in bed for the evening, Bob and Lori sat in the living room. Lori didn't know what was coming, so she prepared herself for the worst.

"I guess I kind of figured he was leaving me, and I was getting ready to deal with that, to be a single mom raising three kids," Lori says quietly. "Like I said, I hadn't been trying to make plans or figure out the future. I was living one day at a time, trying to be a new person with God's help."

Bob told Lori that the affair was over, that it had been stupid, and that he wanted their marriage to work out.

"That was exactly how he said it," Lori remembers. "He didn't apologize to me. He didn't ask me to forgive him. He didn't explain anything. But there was a serious tone in his voice. He seemed different somehow. He wasn't making excuses or joking around or anything. He was dead serious."

Lori remembers praying silently while her husband was talking, asking God to give her His advice and His guidance. "Bob didn't really make a speech, he just said the affair was over and he wanted our marriage to work out. So after he said that, I told him I wanted the same thing."

Forgiven and Faithful

Lori suggested that they get some marriage counseling, but Bob declined.

"He told me he wanted our marriage to work, but he thought counseling was a crock," Lori tells us. "I hope I don't offend you by saying that. But that's exactly the way he said it to me."

David smiles. "We're not offended," he explains gently, speaking for both of us. Lori continues her story.

"It was maybe a year or so later, and my two oldest kids were in school. Both of them were adjusting well to school. One day Bob came home and said we needed to talk again. It had been a year since I found his note and we had our discussion, and we really hadn't talked much about it since. I know some people would tell me I shouldn't have stayed with him, but I was still busy living one day at a time. I wasn't worrying about Bob, I was totally focused on being the best me that I could possibly be. After a year of doing that, it still took all my energy.

"So one day Bob came home and said we needed to talk. And that night, about a year after the big blow-up, he finally apologized and told me he knew it was wrong while he was doing it. He didn't make any excuses. He didn't give me any details. I am so glad for that—the one note I found had way too many details! I didn't need any more of that to fill up my mind or bother my imagination.

"That night, for the first time since it happened, Bob asked me to forgive him. He told me he wanted our marriage to work and he wanted us to stay together. He told me there wouldn't be any more cheating. Then he said the sweetest thing. He said basically that if I wanted to leave him, he totally understood that. He would never blame me. He would always realize that he was the one who messed up our marriage. But he told me that if I chose to stay with him, he would be faithful. He told me he would understand if I didn't trust him. But whether I trusted him or not, if I stayed around and we stayed together, he would be faithful."

Lori remembers her husband's exact words. "I really mean it," he told her that night. "I'm serious."

For whatever reason, Lori chose to believe him.

"After our conversation that night, I could tell Bob was different. The biggest change I noticed was that he quit flirting with everyone else. He stopped trying to get their attention and make them laugh," Lori says simply.

"He has been so different."

The Biggest Change of All

Meanwhile, by Lori's account, the real changes have been in her.

"I think I was prepared to live alone. I think I expected our marriage to end back then. I mean, I wouldn't have stayed with a man who was cheating on me. I wouldn't have lived in a marriage where my husband was having sex with other people. So I think I was prepared to live alone and raise my kids alone.

"All I did was live one day at a time, letting God change my heart. And about a year later, I guess God changed Bob's heart too.

"He doesn't talk much about things like that. He is very private about his spiritual side. To this day, I don't even know whether God worked on him or whether he got wiser and more mature. I don't have any explanation. I just know that he behaves differently. He's a great dad to our kids. Our three neighbors moved out, which is a great thing, but Bob was already keeping very different boundaries with them even before they left.

"Bob is different, my marriage is different, my kids are doing better...all of that is true," Lori says. "And all of it happened because God humbled me enough to see what *my* problems were and how *I* needed to repent."

Lori pauses. "I think I'm done," she tells us. "Anyway, that's pretty much the same story I told Heather the day we talked. And I guess now you know why Heather and I connected so fully in that moment."

All four of us look around the coffee shop, suddenly conscious of time. We've been here for almost two hours, and it's felt like perhaps five minutes or so. Twice during our time together David has gotten up to refill our ice waters or to bring us additional napkins. Tables around us have filled and emptied. People have come and gone. In the midst of that, two marriage counselors and two married women have shared a conversation about love and life.

It's been a conversation about what happens when God gets permission to work in a woman's heart. It's been a confession about what happens when women repent, seek God's forgiveness, and begin to change their ways with God's help.

All of this is good in its own right and more than enough cause for celebration. Yet this has also been a conversation about the change that can happen in a husband when his wife yields her heart to God and begins a new walk with Him.

"Thank you," David tells these women a few minutes later.

I express my thanks by hugging each of them, and they each warmly embrace me in return.

The sun is slanting across the bridge as we join heavy traffic across the San Francisco–Oakland Bay Bridge again. Both David and I are quiet in the car, which is rare for us. We drive in silence for a few minutes, watching the birds above and the bay below us. Both of us are lost in thought.

"Just look what's possible," David finally says. "Just look what can happen when God breaks through in one partner's life. Look how changing one person can bring change to a whole environment: marriage, family, and home."

I marvel at this also. I want to say something wise or appropriate, something serious and helpful. But at this moment I am still caught up in Heather's and Lori's stories. All I can say is, "God is good."

He reaches across the car and squeezes my hand.

"Yes, He is," my husband agrees.

8

Outcomes, Parts 1 and 2

I n chapters 2 through 6, we introduced you to five wives who hoped for better days in their marriage relationships. As you got to know these women, you may have found that you have a lot in common with some of them. Marriages face the same challenges the world over. We humans come in all shapes and sizes and colors, but the things that make us human don't change. Wherever you travel, the challenges of making a marriage and forming a family are surprisingly similar. We're all in this together.

In these three final chapters we'll see what happened when these five women invited God to help change *them*—not their life partners or their marriage relationships. Each of these women came face-to-face with her own reflection, and each one made a challenging but positive choice to deal with the woman in the mirror and not the man in the den.

You may be surprised to see how a change in these women began to produce changes in the men they married. Case by case, we'll briefly explore how the marriage relationship benefited when the woman took a penitent, teachable, humble approach to her conversation with God.

Could you become a new person and yet still be trapped in the same old relational problems? Yes, absolutely. Could you experience a "godly woman makeover" and yet still be married to a Neanderthal who refuses to help make things better? Yes, of course. There are no guarantees in these pages, no formulas or easy steps you can take to transform your husband. We hope this book will lead to a makeover in your own heart. Becoming a godly woman is its own reward.

Yet you are likely to find that the change in you produces a change in the man you married. You will probably discover that a positive improvement in your attitude, your tone, your conversation, and your conduct produces corresponding positive improvements in your marriage. Many have found it so, including the wives we profile here.

Will you discover these same possibilities in your own situation? As we write these words, we pray that you will. We invite a God who performs miracles to invade your marriage relationship with His grace, His mercy, and His healing power. We offer you the chance to open yourself to God's transforming power within your own heart, your own spirit, your own mind.

Even if your marriage never changes, may the change in you produce a beautiful harvest among your family and friends. May your office or neighborhood or congregation be a brighter and healthier place because of who you are.

Who you are matters, now and always.

Outcome 1: Unspoken Expectations

In chapter 2 we introduced you to a couple who could star in a film called *Clueless in California*. Brent and Carrie were five years into their marriage when suddenly their relationship hit the wall and their marriage almost ended.

It is not uncommon for marriages to experience a crash and burn during the first three to seven years of the relationship. Our original expectations and our actual experiences may begin to clash, perhaps violently. We discover that marriage is not what we expected. We are busier, more alone, less happy, less fulfilled...our perceptions may vary, but the common denominator is a huge gap between our dreams of marriage and the way things are working out in our real lives.

This disillusionment gap can occur in both genders, but it's usually most painful for the wife. She's the one who is likely to have spent much of her life dreaming about being married and picturing herself in an idealized future. She's the one who may discover that the dirty diapers and the high credit card bills don't match the dreams and the hopes she had for being married.

Carrie had very high expectations of Brent's behavior toward her. She had grown up with a caring and attentive father who loved his wife and expressed that love verbally and with frequent surprise gifts. Carrie based her view of marriage on what she had seen growing up. She saw a wife who thrived on her husband's attention, flourishing in an atmosphere of positive affirmation, romantic touches, and constant attention.

Five years into her own marriage, Carrie saw none of these good behaviors in Brent. Instead, she felt trapped at home raising two little boys all by herself. Brent was almost an absentee father, frequently away from home for long periods of time. He forgot their anniversaries and her birthdays. He never surprised her with roses or chocolates, let alone handmade cards. To say the least, he fell short of the high standards Carrie's dad had set. She began to believe she had simply married the wrong man and that starting over might be her wisest choice.

Yet here's the key issue. Carrie had never described her dad's behavior to Brent—not while they were dating, not during their brief episodes of premarital counseling, and not during the five years since they had said "I do." She had never explained to Brent how she thought marriage would be and particularly how she thought a husband should treat his wife. Her stylized, idealized view of marriage was locked inside her own mind. She never brought it out and shared it with Brent.

Carrie had exceptionally high expectations for husbands. It's safe to say that Carrie's father is unusually attentive, creative, and generous in his behavior toward his wife. He was the only model Carrie had ever seen close-up, so she naturally assumed that all husbands brought home flowers, created handwritten cards, and caressed their wives with sappy attention. She assumed that all husbands knew the power of an unexpected gift at an unexpected time.

A pearl necklace on a random Tuesday?

"Oh—you shouldn't have!" (But of course, yes, you should have.)

Same Game, Different Scorecards

Carrie used a clearly defined scorecard to evaluate Brent's performance and the success of their marriage. She had assembled the scorecard while growing up in her own family. As an adult, day after day, she mentally compared Brent's behavior with her dad's behavior. Time after time, the box score at the end of the day would read something like "Dad—5, Brent—0."

Carrie was consistently disappointed by Brent's poor performance, and believed she had somehow just chosen the wrong man. She had even considered setting her first choice aside and starting over.

Carrie describes those first few years of her marriage: "All of my illusions were shattering at once." She had hoped to pursue graduate school, but then the babies started coming. Unconsciously, she blamed her husband. The pregnancies were his fault, and so was her loss of graduate school.

Meanwhile, Brent was busy achieving and succeeding outside the home. He was racking up big sales gains and advancing in his career, receiving accolades and awards, higher pay, and frequent bonuses. Yet the respect that Brent received so freely and so frequently at work was missing when he walked through the doors of his own home at the end of a busy day.

"I was getting it done," Brent says proudly, talking about his sales success at the time. "It was like I was on fire. Everything I tried seemed to succeed."

Yet on Carrie's hidden scorecard, Brent was failing. She evaluated her husband according to a concealed list of qualities and traits she expected in a husband. Based on those invisible standards, Brent was washing out as a spouse. He may have been getting it done at work, but regardless of what he thought, he was definitely *not* getting it done at home.

Brent had his own internal way of keeping score in the marriage. He was providing for his family, climbing the ladder of economic and financial success, and winning awards for his competence as a salesman. On Brent's scorecard, he was a huge winner as a husband. *Any wife would be blessed to have a husband like me*, he thought to himself. *I'm the man. Look at my salary, my standard of living, and my upward mobility.*

These two intelligent people were sharing the same home and yet making radically different judgments and evaluations. They were sharing the same experiences together yet responding to those experiences quite differently. They had hugely conflicting interpretations of how they were doing as a couple and as a family.

Do you see why this couple could be *Clueless in California*?

"I didn't even know we had a problem," Brent says. Carrie is frustrated, angry, upset, and ready to call it quits. Yet Brent thinks things are fine. Since he's mostly happy with their arrangement, he assumes everyone else is too. Sex is okay, the kids are okay, the wife is okay...what's not to like here? Brent feels good about his priorities and believes he's doing the right things as a husband.

Two very different scorecards are tracking the success or failure of this marriage. Not surprisingly, the scores are vastly different. So is Brent winning or losing? Let's check the scorecards.

Carrie's says, "My husband is a total failure."

Brent's says: "I'm succeeding as a husband. Check me out!"

Welcome to the dangerous trap of unspoken expectations.

Speaking Up Makes a Big Difference

Happily, the outcome for this couple is positive. When Brent and Carrie's marriage hit the wall, they realized that one of their main problems was that Carrie brought a lot of unspoken expectations into their relationship. While Brent was busy achieving and succeeding according to his own internal but somewhat misguided criteria, Carrie was busy judging and condemning him on the basis of her own internal and somewhat unrealistic values.

Once Carrie began to explain what her values were, Brent knew what he had to do in order to measure up. They began using matching scorecards. Brent, greatly to his credit, responded by stepping up with his A game. He started being the kind of husband Carrie had always secretly expected. He swung all the way from clueless underachiever to proactive overachiever. He began caring about birthdays, remembering anniversaries, and dreaming up bigger and more dramatic ways to celebrate these events. He even bought a greeting card that was about four feet high! It was the most expensive anniversary card in the store, which is why he purchased it for Carrie and brought it home on their big day. He wasn't trying to be the second-best husband in the world. He wasn't hoping to bunt safely and get on base. Brent wanted to hit a home run, win the ball game, and be the hero.

As it turns out, Brent wanted to succeed as a husband just as much as he wanted to succeed at work. He just started out not knowing how to do that on Carrie's hidden terms. For all he knew in the beginning, he was already an exceptional catch. He was earning a lot, providing well, doing well at work, and moving forward in every category. Who knew that you also needed to be remembering dates, purchasing flowers, and surprising your wife from time to time? Who knew?

Not Brent. But once he found out, he got in the game. Male to the core, he didn't come to play. He came to win. Brent stepped up and became an attentive, creative, affectionate husband to Carrie. In fact, he did all of these things with his own typical over-the-top flair.

"Once I knew I had to measure up to her dad, that wasn't good enough for me," Brent chuckles as he recalls those early efforts. "I didn't want to catch up to the guy, I wanted to pass him and leave him in the dust!" Spoken like a true male.

Many husbands are wired much like Brent. They naturally compare and compete. They boast and brag to each other, always trying to win. They want to be successes as husbands, but they aren't aware of the standards their wives use to judge them. Once they know the standards, they're off to the races, ready to achieve and succeed.

They want to score, to win, and to be noticed for achieving these things.

Now Comes Mirror Time

So what about your marriage? Are you avoiding the trap of unspoken expectations? Are you steering clear of the pitfalls of unexpressed hopes and standards? Or are you judging and condemning your husband because he fails to do something he should have? Are you secretly disappointed because he does some things the wrong way or at the wrong time? If so, you may be more deeply enmeshed in the expectations trap than you realize.

"He should just know," wives tell us. "Anybody should know this stuff." But these women seem to think all men should come from the factory with a full set of instructions to follow so that they would already know how to be good husbands.

Well, first of all, men don't receive these instructions at birth.

Second, if they did, do you think they'd read them? Most guys tear into projects and start building. Directions are for later, when you discover a few missing parts and you're trying to decide how important they are. Instructions? They're optional.

Maybe all men should know proper etiquette, good table manners, and the daily duties of a romantic husband, but many guys don't. The odds are pretty good that the man you married hasn't already studied your version of the perfect husband so he can measure up. Raised in his own family of origin, looking at the models he saw while growing up, your husband has his own internal set of values that describe how he ought to behave. He's living by his own code, not by yours. And if you don't already know this by now, you'd probably be surprised by the difference between his scorecard and yours.

As our final thought for this outcome, here's a handy tip from Carrie, who has emerged from her experiences as a happy and fulfilled wife and also a frequent leader of women's groups. These days, no one would believe she almost gave up, walked out on her husband, and bailed on her marriage.

Carrie has done some speaking at women's events at her church and has taught classes for new moms as part of the church's outreach to the community. She shares freely from her own wisdom, and she's open and up-front about the mistakes she believes she made as a younger wife. So here's a tip from Carrie the teacher.

"Please understand the difference between communicating your unspoken expectations, which is hugely helpful, and nagging your husband, which is quite unproductive, as you'll see for yourself," Carrie implores. "If you want something to go undone for a long time," she suggests with a smile, "just nag your husband about it incessantly."

Her point is well taken. Nothing in this section should be construed as saying that the best way to communicate with your husband is by giving him orders or constantly badgering him about chores undone, projects unfinished, or calendar items coming up ahead. Nagging or badgering your husband is likely to do more harm than to help.

As with almost anything you hope to communicate effectively, timing is everything. And if communication has broken down, or it's not a strong suit for you and your husband, by all means sit down with a counselor so you can talk about these things as calmly and appropriately as possible.

Get the Referee in the Game

Counselors can be of immense value to a couple, allowing the husband and wife to communicate more clearly and more directly while avoiding anger and defensiveness. If you attend a small church, you may find that your minister is available to you without cost. Try telling your pastor that you'd like to sit down with him or her and work to make your marriage better. You'll make your pastor's day!

Larger churches often have teams that attend to the counseling or pastoral care issues. The advantage of a larger church is simple. If you don't have a positive experience with your first attempt at finding a counselor, you've got several other options.

Never be worried or ashamed if you go to a counselor and things just don't seem to click and move forward. Instead of giving up on counseling itself, just try meeting with another person. Going through two or three false starts is worth the effort if you can end up with an attentive, respectful, nonjudgmental helper. Good counselors will help the two of you express your opinions, unlock your unspoken expectations, and make progress in ways that both of you can see and appreciate.

Just remember, expectations that go unspoken also tend to go unmet. Speak up—at the right times and in positive ways—and let your husband know about your hopes and dreams for your marriage.

Outcome 2: Unrecognized Pride

Maria and Perry's larger-than-life, picture-perfect home would tempt many of us to be covetous. But when Maria opened her mouth, we realized that this wealthy woman had exactly the same kinds of problems that the rest of us deal with. She may live in a different neighborhood, but she's got the same issues. Money truly does not buy happiness—although many of us would be willing to learn this lesson by experience!

As Maria talked about Perry during our initial encounter, she said he wasn't helping, wasn't contributing, and wasn't trying. Maria was unaware of the irony of her words. She was literally surrounded by proof of Perry's success, the evidence of his love for her, and the fruit of his attentiveness to his family's needs. Yet Maria's report didn't take that into account.

"I'm the only one who is trying to make this work."

"I'm the only one of us who cares about this relationship."

"I'm the only one who cares about the kids."

"I'm the only one who does any of the chores around here."

In these and a dozen other ways, Maria repeated the same litany to us as we sat in her high-dollar kitchen. Maria's song included a recurring motif: "I'm the only one…"

She Was Right—Is That So Wrong?

Let's candidly admit that Maria's perspective about her life was not entirely wrong. Day after day, only Maria drove her kids where they needed to go, read them stories at night, and took care of their other needs. Only Maria cooked the meals, washed the laundry, and cleaned the house. (She may have had a housekeeper, but let's not get technical.)

Maria's perceptions were basically accurate. Perry was gone a lot, busily achieving major financial success. He was carrying the weight of their standard of living, but he wasn't doing a lot to care emotionally for his wife, raise the children, or fix things around the house. So Maria's perspective was somewhat based on fact.

The problem, however, is that in Maria's inner dialogue, she had become heroic and noble and worthy of respect while Perry had become a miserable failure. Maria, filled with self-pity and an exaggerated sense of her own honor and accomplishments, saw herself as the heroine of her family drama. Perry was the villain. To Maria, these issues were black and white, simple and concrete. She was in the right, and he was in the wrong.

The Story from Your Neighborhood

When your husband isn't cooperating, helping, or responding the way you hoped he would, the most dangerous trap in the world is to start believing that you're in the right and he's in the wrong. This clear-cut and simplistic explanation gives you the moral high ground. Left unchecked, it can become a full-blown martyr complex. You suffer nobly as your husband fails and falls short. You are being responsible and steady and committed and helpful to the worthless man you married.

The more these feelings are based on facts, the more dangerous the temptation becomes. Without knowing it, you become prideful about the wonderful way you're behaving in your relationship. You're the hero, the noble martyr. You're worth of respect, and before you know it, you're the president of your own fan club. And pride goes before...

Maria allowed God to change her heart, and she did so with humility and grace. Once she got a good look at the woman in the mirror, she resolved to change her attitude, change her behavior, and change her direction. Maria's courage allowed great things to begin. She began noticing, appreciating, and valuing Perry's contributions. She began to pay him unexpected compliments at unexpected times. She became the president of her husband's fan club, not her own.

And these behaviors on Maria's part *preceded* any visible change in her spouse.

This may be one of the most important truths we communicate to you in this book. Maria did not change her attitude *because* her husband behaved better. Instead, Maria changed her attitude *before* her husband behaved better. There is a world of difference.

A New Woman Produces New Results

Maria changed her attitude because God changed her heart. She decided that whether Perry ever did any housework, helped the kids with their homework, or romanced her with dinner and a movie, she was going to be a positive, encouraging, and supportive wife. She was going to value what she had and not whine about what she lacked.

"I had been whining and complaining for a long time—maybe not to others, but in my own spirit," Maria says today, greatly changed. "I had been feeling sorry for myself, which is never constructive or useful. Until the day I received a big shock in my kitchen, I had been spending a lot of time feeling sorry for my kids, feeling sorry for me... just feeling sorry in general. I felt like my kids were being cheated out of a father. I felt like I was being cheated out of a husband.

"I focused on how unfair that was. I didn't realize that my tone, attitude, conversation, and behavior were all so negative. Later I looked back and realized that some of my good friends started spending less time with me, which I hadn't noticed at the time. Now I realize that they probably backed away from me, at least unconsciously, because I whined so much. I wouldn't want to be around me either if I was like that!"

Maria is 180 degrees different from her former self, and she understands fully that the changes in her were not guaranteed to impact her marriage or change her husband. However, by the grace of God, that is exactly what happened. Maria's story is in this book for that reason.

Romancing the Stone: Melting the Husband's Heart

This is how it happened. First, Maria let God change her heart and spirit. She became positive, appreciative, supportive, and encouraging. She made these changes without seeing any changes in her situation.

Next, as Maria became an encouraging wife, Perry began coming home early and taking time off. His behavior and habits changed profoundly *after* he saw the change in Maria.

"He comes home early almost every Friday now," Maria says. "He leaves the office after lunch and just doesn't go back in. He tells me that most of his peers are out drinking anyway, so they won't notice his absence at the office."

Maria is positively beaming. "I can't tell you how much the kids look forward to Daddy coming home now. For a while there, they didn't even know who Daddy was! Now they spend time with him most evenings, and on Fridays he gets home from work at about the same time they get home from school."

Perry has discovered the joy of being at home. He is noticeably more active in his children's lives. He is definitely more involved in caring for his wife and participating in her life. He's the same person and yet a whole new man. Maria couldn't be happier. Today her smile is as wide as the Grand Canyon.

We can't promise you these same results, but we can promise you this: Becoming a godly woman is its own reward. Let that become your mantra and your motto. Print it on your heart and your mirror or your fridge. Instead of waiting for circumstances to change or your husband to magically improve, start allowing God to have control of your emotions, leadership of your attitudes, and direction over your speech and conversation. As God makes the changes He has in mind for you, you will become what author Elizabeth George calls "a woman after God's own heart."

A Clear Pattern

Although Maria's story is dramatic and refreshing, stories like hers are more common than you might think. Time after time, David and I watch in awe as God changes a woman's heart and then begins to change her husband.

We have watched some of the most lost and misguided husbands do complete U-turns after their wives hit their knees in prayer, let God have control of their hearts, and became new creatures in Him. Somehow the fragrant aroma of a transformed wife permeates the whole house, finding its way into even a husband's hardened heart.

Men tend to have a great sense of smell. When the fragrance of a changed woman is in the house, men perk up and take notice. This is not a promise, but it is a trend. It's not an exception; it's a pattern. It's an outcome that could, by the grace of God, invade your home also.

Are you ready to begin? Here are some thoughts you can use to get started.

Reflections for Your Personal Journey

1. Are you avoiding the pitfalls of unspoken expectations? Are you ready to quit judging your husband (and others) by a hidden standard? Do you understand why expectations that go unexpressed also tend to go unmet?

2. If your husband is faltering or letting you down, is there any chance that you've become prideful about your own responsible, committed behavior as a wife? Have you seen this situation in such good-versus-evil terms that somehow you now believe yourself to be holier, wiser, or better than you really are?

3. Are you ready to let God hold a mirror in front of you so you can see your true heart, true attitudes, and true emotions? Are you ready to change, even if nothing in your situation or your marriage changes?

4. Are you ready to memorize and live by the mantra that becoming a godly woman is its own reward? Instead of trying to change and manipulate the world you live in, are you ready to become clay in the hands of a potter God?

9

Outcomes, Parts 3 and 4

Outcome 3: Unrelenting Criticism

We are writing these words during the NBA playoffs. This part of the basketball season reminds us so vividly of our encounter with Jerry and Darlene in Phoenix. They kindly invited us over for dinner and a Celtics playoff game. But as you may remember, when the game began, so did a sudden outburst of relational fireworks. Darlene interrupted a wonderfully relaxing evening with her insistence that we work on their marriage problems. She actually meant, "I want to criticize Jerry for all the things he's doing wrong."

As Darlene began her tirade, we calmly interrupted, interjected, intervened, and in every way tried to channel and contain her critical spirit, but she continued to call out Jerry by listing his failures and all the ways he was disappointing her. Greatly to his credit, Jerry did not try to fight back. Although he had plenty of opportunities to become defensive and lash out against Darlene, this gentle giant managed to contain himself and behave very well.

Every once in a while, Jerry tried to claim some points for a good thing he had done or a compromise he'd made for Darlene's sake. But his words barely left his mouth before Darlene interrupted to point out that he'd fallen short, missed the mark, and disappointed her yet again. It wasn't enough. It wasn't the right time. It was worse than doing nothing.

She must have been saving up these accusations for a long time. For whatever reason, she was a flowing fountain of volcanic anger. In just a few moments, her critical spirit filled the beautiful outdoor gazebo-like structure with so much ash and lava. An evening that had started in such a promising way quickly devolved into overt hostility and name-calling.

Two Referees and Lots of Whistles

David and I took turns that night defending Jerry—not because we were taking sides, but merely to maintain some rules of engagement for couples who need to vent. Counselors are very handy in situations like this because they're trained to help couples communicate without destroying each other. Counselors are like referees. Their role is to keep people from committing fouls.

We had our hands full on this particular evening. Every word Darlene spoke had massive capacity for destruction. We kept interrupting, calming her down, and keeping the conversation from going out-of-bounds. But despite our constant efforts, the pattern kept recurring.

Perhaps Darlene was hearing impaired. She could not or would not learn even the most basic lessons about how to speak wisely to or about her husband. She kept repeating her patterns of criticism, accusation, and name-calling as she spelled out the many ways Jerry was disappointing her. She would not be calmed or satisfied.

Where Husbands Go When They Hurt

David was very quiet as we drove back to our hotel that night. "I think he's having an affair," he said softly. "He didn't tell me so, and I sure hope I'm wrong, but everything points to that."

David is naturally intuitive and often knows things no one could possibly know. We talked for a few minutes about the husband's demeanor. "I hope I'm wrong," David repeated, "but he acts like a man who has already checked out of the relationship. He behaved tonight like a guy who has already found some consolation somewhere else. He seems resigned to the fact that his wife can't be satisfied. I sure hope he's not getting his own satisfaction elsewhere."

Take My Wife—Please

When a wife profoundly disrespects her husband, when he feels as if she disregards and undervalues even his best efforts, he becomes vulnerable to more encouraging persons and situations. Someone at work may laugh at his joke on a lunch break. Someone he cares about may need help with marriage problems. His motivations may be harmless or even commendable, but the situation is dangerous because of his unmet needs for respect and appreciation.

One way or another, when a wife profoundly disrespects her husband, he is vulnerable to outside influences in a way he might not otherwise be. A woman who listens to him, laughs at his humor, compliments him on the job, congratulates him on some achievement...such a woman becomes an enormous positive contrast with the complaining, criticizing presence at home.

A husband in such a case goes home slowly, goes home less often, spends more time away from home, and may ultimately stray into an affair. He may not have intended to go there, but he finds himself there soon enough. The pattern repeats itself constantly.

This is not to remove responsibility from the husband. Comedian Flip Wilson built a career on the phrase "the devil made me do it!" It was funny when Flip said it because he always trotted out that line as an excuse for any of his bad behavior. But we are not giving husbands any right to justify an affair by saying, "My wife made me do it." No excuse can justify breaking your vows or backing out of your promises. Most affairs do not begin at gunpoint. The husband has a choice, and he makes it. He is fully responsible for his own wrong behavior and its consequences.

But when a husband lives in a hostile, negative, critical, demeaning environment, he becomes vulnerable and open to situations that are positive and encouraging. Beaten down at home, he is vulnerable to being built up almost anywhere else. This does not give him a free pass to cheat on his wife, but it weighs him down with an increased receptivity to positive, affirming people, including other women.

And let's face it, plenty of women in the world are just waiting to be positive and encouraging to a depressed husband whose wife does not appreciate, value, and respect him. The world is full of such women.

Even Big Boys Need Respect

To get a better idea of how your words affect your husband, consider the way you talk to your children. If you repeatedly tell a child he is clumsy, he is much more likely to believe you and trip over his feet, fall down frequently, and knock things over. He will live down to your opinion of him, bumbling his way through life.

If you tell a child she is stupid, she may have trouble learning. The more you tell her how stupid she is, the more likely she is to believe your opinion. Even if she consciously resists and argues with you, at an unconscious level she tends to become what you see in her. She may start performing poorly at school, fall lower in her grades, and begin to believe that although other people can learn, she cannot. After all, she tells herself internally, she's stupid. She heard that from you, and even if she wants to disagree, something inside her remembers it. Powerful emotions get attached to the message that she is stupid or unworthy.

This is why unrelenting criticism is so damaging. Criticism interferes with more than our conscious thinking and active mental processes. Criticism gets down deep and messes with our self-esteem, our subconscious, the deepest places within us. Criticism begins to mold us and shape us in its own negative ways and patterns.

After more than two decades of counseling troubled marriages, we can tell you that many husbands began to stray because their wives constantly accused them of cheating. Having not yet begun an affair, they crossed over because they were being criticized and accused of it constantly. "If she already thinks I'm guilty anyway," many husbands have told us, "I might as well get the benefits." Although we know cheating brings no real benefits, we understand what these husbands are saying. "If you find me guilty, I might as well actually *be* guilty."

Are we excusing these husbands for their sinful and immature choices? Heaven forbid. We're simply explaining that some men end up having affairs not because they are oversexed or natural predators, but because the lack of respect at home leaves them vulnerable to others who seem more supportive. Of course, these others who seem more supportive are often home wreckers.

Words Have Power and Consequences

Attacks, accusations, and criticisms shape people's character and self-image. The closer our relationships with people, the more access we have to them, the more frequent our interactions…the more potential damage we can do to their self-worth and behavior. A cheating husband is personally responsible for his own behavior, but we should acknowledge that some husbands are pushed in destructive directions by a corrosive, negative pattern of unrelenting criticism.

Are these husbands justified in having affairs? Of course not! But do you understand why they might drift off in those directions? Do you understand how they would enjoy being around someone who laughed openly, lived lightly, and encouraged them a little bit?

We Hope for the Best

As we write, Jerry and Darlene are still together. They've begun seeing a local marriage counselor, and they report that they are making some progress. We do not know whether Jerry is involved outside his marriage. David retains his intuitive sense that this is so. Because of his hunch, both of us are praying that the affair, if indeed there is one, is soon broken off and that Jerry returns to his marriage in full faithfulness. In other situations, we've seen affairs ended, marriages healed, and broken families restored—all because God answers prayer!

Meanwhile, step-by-step Darlene is getting some clues about the damage she has done with her unrelenting criticism. As far as we can tell, she does not yet realize how powerfully destructive she has been over the course of several years of marriage. Is she responsible for her husband's affair, if in fact he's having one? No, she does not bear direct responsibility. Yet has her behavior made her husband more vulnerable to the possibility of having an affair? Has her behavior left her husband susceptible to others' appreciation and support? Sadly, yes.

The Power of Praise Time

If you are using your words to build up and encourage your husband, you are giving him a strong first line of defense against extramarital affairs. Your husband is much less vulnerable to others' appreciation if you are actively, aggressively, powerfully, and positively affirming him and building him up at home. Your affirmation creates a zone of protection around your husband. When you value and respect him, you are meeting some of his most basic male needs.

Conversely, a man is much more vulnerable to an affair if he is subjected to unrelenting criticism at home. Before long he dreads walking in the door of his own house. He finds other pathways to walk, and he begins frequenting welcoming places where he is more apparently valued and respected. He is responsible for these choices, but the sad news is that under these kinds of conditions, he is much more likely to make the wrong choice.

The simple truth is this: To go back and retract the hurtful and negative things you've said in the past is very difficult. To suddenly backpedal after you've criticized a person is rarely effective. The initial insult is felt far more deeply than any subsequent efforts to make up or apologize.

Therefore, the best thing you can do is avoid the trap of unrelenting criticism altogether. Listen to yourself very carefully and determine whether your language and tone are usually negative or positive. Being a negative and critical person opens the door to a whole range of destructive possibilities. Being a positive and encouraging person creates a hedge of protection and almost always leads to better outcomes and happier places.

Outcome 4: Unhelpful Gossip

Chapter 5 included the word *pornography*. It's one of those words that grabs your attention and remains in your brain. A very helpful book called *Every Man's Battle* tackles the issue of men's struggles to stay pure even though pornography is readily available and invasively spreading into our homes and offices.

Increasingly, pornography is available not only to adults but also to kids with access to a computer. Where once a straying husband might have needed valid ID to enter a so-called adult bookstore, now the Internet is flowing 24/7 with sights and sounds that are highly pornographic. Despite efforts to restrict access, much of this pornography is readily available to the young and curious. More and more, this is not so much every man's battle as it is every person's battle.

There's a Reason This Isn't a Picture Book

You will remember that a young wife came home and found her husband paying a lot of attention to naked women on the television. The women happened to be well-endowed and probably not merely by their Creator. Remember how this young wife, so distraught and so confused by what she encountered, began seeking help from others? And in order to receive that help, she first had to describe the problem. She had to let people know what she had suffered before she could get their advice.

Melody was upset, just as anyone else would be under these circumstances, so she shared her secret with a trusted friend. This wasn't a rumor. After all, she had caught Jarrod in the very act! So often we regard something as gossip only if it's untrue. In reality, the juiciest gossip has at least some elements of truth in it. Gossip is more powerful and more damaging when it contains a least a little bit of the truth, perhaps twisted a bit to make it more interesting.

Melody's trusted friend may not have told the whole world. More likely, she just told one or two of her own trusted friends. But then those trusted friends each told a few of their trusted friends. This is how gossip spreads: Each person probably made certain that whenever she shared her secret, she stressed that the information was confidential. But very soon, the whole church knew about it.

"I Have a Prayer Concern to Share with You"

Does this remind you of any churches you've attended or stories you've heard?

There is enormous power in beginning your story, "Now this is confidential, so don't tell anyone." You immediately gain your listener's attention. Her ears perk up with sudden interest. If you want people's full attention, just give them a hint that what you're sharing is highly confidential. They may have been drifting off before, but now they're with you. What's up? What are you about to share?

Particularly in smaller churches, where everyone tends to know everyone else's business anyway, the destructive power of gossip is amazing. But remaining quiet is apparently not an option for some people, so they preface their remarks in the most spiritual way possible. "I have a prayer request you should know about." After all, if we're going to pray for this poor distraught wife, shouldn't we get a clear description of what her husband was watching?

After Melody shared her secret with her friend, she also told someone in her family. She made a seemingly wise choice by confiding in a trusted older sister. Anyone who has an older sister is greatly blessed—older sisters can be fountains of wisdom. They experience puberty, start dating, get married, and have babies before we do. No wonder so many of us women turn to our older sisters when we have questions or problems.

Yet in this case, the trusted older sister made a huge mistake. For some reason, she told the mom. And for some reason, the mom told the dad. Suddenly the family circle was contaminated with too much information, and this churchgoing family with solid religious values was passing judgment on the unworthy new husband who had married in.

People assumed the dad was thinking, *I knew he wasn't good enough for her.* Maybe the mom was thinking it too. Maybe the sisters and the brothers and the nieces and the nephews were thinking it too. Should we call Grandma, just to be sure she knows?

Setting aside the transgression for a moment, would *you* want to be the husband in that setting, with an entire family circle looking at you accusingly? Wouldn't you feel like the only evil person in a room filled with saints?

But Her Difficulty Was Real, Wasn't It?

Reading about this situation, we can easily understand why Melody was distraught. Especially for a churchgoing woman married to a churchgoing man, coming home to find big breasts on the big screen can cause big problems.

It's something you don't expect. It immediately messes with the way you think about your husband and your marriage. It undermines your feelings of security. You begin to question your own attractiveness. You begin to wonder about the man you married. In a case like this, seeking counsel and advice makes perfect sense.

The problem here wasn't that Melody sought counsel; it was that she sought in the wrong places. Let's be candid. Most of our trusted friends have passed along other people's secrets to us, probably more than once. So most of our trusted friends have probably also passed along our secrets to others more than once. Don't we already know that, even before we talk to our closest friends?

In this case the damaging secret was about Jarrod. Melody told a friend something negative about him, her friend told another friend who told another friend…and soon his reputation in the family and in the church was destroyed. Jarrod and Melody eventually decided to leave Boise and start over in British Colombia.

We found them there, sipping coffee in West Vancouver, wondering if they would repeat the same damaging patterns. David privately worked with Jarrod on the issue of pornography. Jarrod claimed that pornography wasn't a problem for them, but in fact, it has had a highly corrosive effect on many marriage relationships.

But Jarrod and Melody wanted to meet with us because they were both concerned that Melody would repeat the pattern of sharing unhelpful gossip, which led to their sudden exodus from their home. As we spoke and counseled together, it was clear that she needed to set better boundaries around some topics of conversation. As we talked about these things, we could almost sense lightbulbs starting to glow in Melody's mind. She began to see where and how to draw the boundaries as she talked about the issues and challenges of her marriage.

Speak Up, Walk Out, Get Help

Melody clearly needed to learn where to seek counsel for important issues. Nowhere in this book will we argue against older sisters or condemn trusted friends. Instead, we'll talk about the importance of guarding someone's reputation, especially if that person is your husband.

Be very clear: We are not talking about remaining in a situation where you are experiencing violence or harm. We are not asking you to stay in that relationship quietly in order to protect your husband. That is the opposite of what we would counsel. When you are not safe in your marriage, you should find safety. You should work on your marriage, with qualified help, from a safe place. No one is asking you to remain quiet, keep on being hurt, and thus protect an abusive husband's reputation. Be clear about that. This is not a book about domestic violence or about being someone's punching bag in order to protect his reputation in the church or the family.

Have You Lived a Perfect Life? Has Anyone?

In this section we are talking about the harm we can do to a person's reputation and their standing in a church or a family when our own loose talk or unhelpful gossip causes them to lose face or to lose the respect of others. How would you feel if the most embarrassing mistake you ever made was suddenly passed around the family table at Thanksgiving? Would you be eager to return at Christmastime? No, you would be ashamed and embarrassed, and you would probably prefer not to go back there for a while.

That is why we are asking you to set aside Jarrod's transgression for a moment (though no one is defending his actions) and focus instead on the damage that his reputation suffered. You might be thinking, *Well, he should have thought of that before he dialed up the naked cheerleaders on his big-screen TV.* You're correct, but that's beside the point. A husband's mistake does not need to be the ruin of his reputation in a church or in a family. Have you never spoken one unwholesome word? Have you never watched part of an unhealthy program? Have you never read part of an unhelpful book?

Most of us feel ashamed about mistakes we have made in one category or another. The Bible reminds us, "All of us have sinned. All of us fall short" (Romans 3:23). We need to remember that we're all human and we all fail. And we'd all prefer that our humiliating mistakes do not become topics of conversation at church or around the dinner table. We'd like our mistakes to be forgiven and forgotten. Maybe it's a courtesy we should extend to others also.

Bad News Sticks like Crazy Glue

The problem with unhelpful gossip is that it makes someone's failure—even a rare or momentary lapse in otherwise good judgment—a defining feature of his or her reputation. Let's say Jarrod got straight A's in graduate school that week, got a big promotion in his job, won some kind of quality control award from his company...and then got caught watching porn on his television. Which one of these facts will be remembered the longest?

Exactly.

Things that are spicy or juicy or interesting tend to linger in our minds long after other things—awards, promotions, or whatever— have faded from memory. Jarrod believes to this day that everyone at the church in Idaho will look at him strangely for the rest of his life. He also believes that his wife's family will never look at him the same way again. Regardless of whether he's right or wrong about that, it's exactly how he feels. Do you understand why he feels this way?

Jarrod stands a pretty good chance of being right about this. Unhelpful gossip can do a lifetime of damage in just a few brief seconds. It can destroy the reputation of a good person, causing him or her to lose respect in a community or church or family. Unhelpful gossip is the last thing on earth you would want hounding you. Therefore, being reminded again of the Golden Rule, it's worth avoiding when it comes to others.

Was Melody wrong to want some advice? Was she crazy to turn to someone older and wiser for help? Not exactly. The problem is that the issues here were not about Melody, but about her husband. And the people she turned to for wise advice and counsel did not manage to keep her secret. And as we've seen, most friends and family members are not particularly adept at keeping secrets.

If you want to trust them with secrets about you, that's up to you because only your own reputation and honor are at stake. If you want to take a risk with your own standing in the community or the church or the family, that's your own risk to take. But if you want to trust people with secrets about someone other than yourself, that's potentially a big mistake about to happen. More than likely you will damage someone's reputation even if you insist that it's highly confidential.

When you need counsel in cases like this, turn to a minister, a priest, a rabbi, a marriage therapist, a family counselor, a school counselor…a professional who is trained and adept at keeping your information safe and confidential. Every once in a long while, a professional will mess up, but that does not invalidate the category. Pastors and counselors are almost always reliable in keeping potentially damaging issues confidential.

Guard other people's reputations. Don't put them at risk in their own circles of family and friends. Even if they are guilty of some offense (such as watching porn on cable), they do not deserve to have their reputation ruined by careless and powerfully destructive gossip.

Reflections for Your Personal Journey

1. Have you ever been around a wife or a husband whose pattern was to criticize his or her spouse? How did it make you feel? Once you recognized the pattern, did you want to spend more time or less time around that person?

2. Were you consistently criticized as a child, perhaps by a parent or an older sibling? If so, how did the criticism make you feel? Did you begin to believe your critics? Did you grow up feeling fat or stupid because someone called you one of those things?

3. Do you realize how easily criticism shapes our own self-image and damages our sense of self-worth? Do you understand that unrelenting criticism wears down a person's confidence, causing him or her to lose hope and perhaps give up?

4. Do you clearly understand why a husband who is criticized at home but respected at work can be vulnerable to outside influences? Can you see how temptation might present itself not as a sexual issue but as an emotional connection with someone who is positive and encouraging?

5. Are you ready to begin building up and encouraging your husband, removing negative and critical words from your arsenal of communication? Do you see why a pattern of being negative can be so dangerous and so damaging?

6. In the section on unhelpful gossip, we talked about pornography. Do you know of marriages that have been negatively impacted by pornography? Do you know of relationships that have ended because one partner had a sexual addiction or was involved in something like Internet porn?

7. As you were reading this story, was your first response to

blame Jarrod for being so stupid, or was your first response to feel sorry for his loss of reputation in his family and his church?

8. If you attend a church regularly, especially a smaller church, do you believe that unhelpful gossip like this would permanently damage someone's reputation? If something is true, can talking about it really be gossip?

9. Have you ever confided in someone you trusted, only to have that person pass along or share what you confided with someone else? How did that make you feel? How would you feel if what was shared was highly negative about you and tended to make other people judge you and condemn you?

10. Do you understand why Jarrod wanted to move away from his church and his wife's family? If you were in this situation, what would you do?

11. If you were advising Melody about her conversations with others, what kinds of helpful tips would you share with her? What does she need to learn about sharing things with others?

12. Do you have access to a pastor, priest, rabbi, or counselor? If you needed to talk to a person in one of these categories, would you know where to look? If you are not a churchgoing person, do you have friends or family members who attend a church and can recommend a minister who will talk with you?

10

Outcomes, Part 5

Outcome 5: Unresolved Bitterness

We've saved this story for last and given it a chapter all by itself because it may be the most exemplary of the stories we've included. Even as we share it, we want to emphasize that we are not promoting a formula for achieving impressive results. Life is complex, and situations are challenging. Most of our difficulties in life are not resolved by quick and easy steps. Nonetheless, we have good reasons for hope.

Beauty and the Beast

We met Sharon at Caribou Coffee, and we listened as she told us her falling-in-love history. She was swept off her feet by a charming and romantic older male. Carl knew how to reach her and what to say. In a fairly short time they progressed from dating to being engaged to living together to being married. Sharon quickly transitioned from being a dependent in a dysfunctional family to living like a full-fledged adult starting a family of her own.

Yet the prince who kissed her started looking more like a frog.

Married (and apparently successful in his quest), Carl began morphing into a lazy, unmotivated, increasingly obese jerk. He didn't make it a priority to locate or keep a job; instead, he bounced from one job to the next, never keeping any employment very long. In between employers he was not exactly a job-hunting fireball. Quite the opposite.

Meanwhile, he let himself go physically. He had been trim and attractive during their courtship. Successfully married, he spent most of his time on the couch, often drinking beer. That's a great way to add excess pounds, especially around the midsection.

Over the course of 20 or 30 years of marriage, one or both partners will commonly add a few pounds. Often a couple gains weight somewhat in tandem. By the time they've been married for 15 or 20 years, each of them may weigh 15 or 20 pounds more than they did on their wedding day. But Carl began to add weight just few months after the wedding. From that point on, his weight ballooned out of control. Only a few years into his marriage relationship, he had added 50 or 60 pounds and hadn't stopped.

When Sharon came home from work (after all, someone had to find and hold onto a job), Carl's body odor filled her house. Are you at all surprised that after working so hard and choosing to be responsible and to keep her appearance attractive, Sharon got a bit angry when Carl became lazy, unmotivated, sloppy, obese, and unwilling to get up off the couch and look for work?

Or are you more surprised that she actually stayed with him through all of this? Would you have stayed with him? Would you have advised your sister or your daughter to stay with him? Would you wish this on your worst enemy? What a great thing to tell a young woman growing up: Maybe someday you can have a husband who eats your groceries, siphons away your income to buy beer, lies around the house all day without taking a shower, and stinks up the whole house with his body odor. Oh, and there's a bonus—he'll get really fat!

This is probably not what most young girls imagine marriage will be like.

Easy to Say

Obviously, from a theological or religious standpoint, you probably advocate that married couples should stay together. But would you follow your own advice if you were in Sharon's place? Many of us have strong convictions about something until we find ourselves in a difficult situation. Suddenly we begin to view things differently. Yes, we're in favor of couples staying together, but like this? Yes, we believe marriage should be permanent, but this kind of marriage?

Would you want your daughter to be the lifelong financial support for a lazy, unmotivated, beer-drinking slob who couldn't hold on to a job? Would you counsel her to stay with this unemployed jerk forever so he could keep getting drunk at your daughter's expense?

Can you be honest with yourself for a moment, as you answer that question?

Moments from Real Life

Well, buckle up because now we're getting around to the outcome.

Sharon was not a Christian during her courtship and wedding. She started dating Carl when she was only 17 years old and moved in with him soon after that. She married him when she turned 18 because in the state where she lived, she was of legal age to marry. She could sign her own certificate without her mother's permission.

Christianity came later. Married for several years, increasingly disillusioned by the reality of her daily life, she walked in the door of a church near her home. Even she isn't certain why she did so.

"They kept sending me stuff in the mail," she tells us over coffee, "and the topics were always interesting. And they'd promise a free meal or dessert or coffee. I kept getting all these mailers, and they always looked interesting, but I never quite got around to going over there and checking out the church.

"I don't know why I finally went. I do know that I got some kind of mailer and something in me just clicked. I just knew that I needed to be in that church. So I walked in not knowing what to expect. Over the next few months I encountered Christ, and He completely changed my life around."

Get the Word Out

She's the reason that churches send out publicity. Here in Southern California, a company called Outreach specializes in helping churches communicate with their communities. They do so with one mission in mind: reaching out to people exactly like Sharon. They help churches connect with people who need an encounter with God but probably aren't otherwise motivated to pursue a spiritual life.

Time after time, we hear true stories from real people that center around a postcard in the mail, a flyer on the doorstep, or something similar. As we listen and explore, we discover that people are struggling with this issue or need help with that problem or are generally frustrated in their lives. Along comes a positive, encouraging, interesting topic on a postcard, and sooner or later, a person, a couple, or an entire family makes their way into a church near their home.

Attending a church is not a magic cure for anything. Yet attending a church in which God's Spirit is present, God's Word is taught, and God's people gather into a grace-filled community—this can change your life.

Sharon is just one of many such examples. Her life permanently changed as a consequence of something she received in the mail from a church she had never visited. In fact, she had not had contact with churches at all while she was growing up. From a distance, her perception was the same that many people share: Churches are full of hypocrites. Churches are places where self-righteous people gather on Sunday in order to judge others and feel superior.

Yet when Sharon finally walked into a church, she found something radically different from what she expected. She found the love of Christ working itself out in the daily lives of a community of imperfect but honest people who gathered together around a common faith and who were learning how faith works itself out in marriages, families, and homes.

Sharon accepted Christ and became a new person. Yet when she returned home to the same old husband, she found herself dealing with the same old anger. She continued to live with him and became even more committed to her marriage because of her newfound religious values. Yet as she stayed with Carl day after day, she became increasingly angry, frustrated, and resentful. Do true Christians actually struggle daily with issues such as anger, frustration, and bitterness in their hearts?

Of course. We all do.

As Sharon was nearing the end of her patience, she finally sought help from some Christian counselors (us). She was finally able to vent some of her pent-up frustration and anger. Instead of holding onto her bitterness, repressing her feelings, or denying her anger, she found a safe and nonjudgmental environment in which she could talk about her struggles.

She poured out her feelings in a stream of consciousness, finally able to just talk to someone about how she felt and what was going on in her marriage. As she did so, she was surprised to realize just how angry she had been. She was surprised at how long she had been angry. She couldn't quite reconcile her faith in God, which was genuine, with the bitterness in her heart. She had already learned that bitterness is a toxic poison that could smother the life of her soul.

Leaning forward in her chair at a Caribou Coffee outlet in St. Paul, Sharon made the health-giving and energizing choice to quit holding on to her unresolved bitterness—to let it go.

The More Things Change...

Driving home from her coffee appointment that day, Sharon noticed a change in her nature and character. Although she continued to see us a few more times, and although she continued to talk about some primary issues and struggles, she found a brand-new peace in her heart. It was a different peace from what she experienced in her conversion, when she received God's grace. This peace is a letting go, a releasing, a healing begun. It's a decision to quit being a storehouse for bitterness and to begin being a cheerful and optimistic wife despite her circumstances—a decision that had been impossible without God's help.

We've saved Sharon's story for last because she—a transformed woman—returned home to a stinky slob in a smelly house, to an overweight beer drinker who couldn't hold a job and wouldn't go looking for one. She drove home to the same situation she was in before, but she was a new person on the inside. She continues counseling and working on her issues, but she is genuinely transformed. She has begun to walk and live and think and act in new ways.

She is no longer a safe depository for bitterness or anger. She is done with that, and she will stay vigilant so that her previous patterns do not recur. She is walking in a new direction now, even in her old circumstances.

And then—amazingly!—her circumstances begin to change.

Sharon is breathless as she speaks about it now. She stops to cry a few times, but these are tears of joy, not frustration. She weeps because she can hardly believe what the power and grace of God has accomplished in her marriage. She cries a bit because she is now a transformed wife who is married to a transformed husband. When Sharon let go of her bitterness and her anger, Carl began to change. This is not an urban legend; this is a true story of a transformed marriage.

As Sharon experienced a new hope and optimism in her personality, a new joy in the place of her former anger, Carl was won over by the dramatic changes in her tone, attitude, and words. The transformation was not instant, and the changes did not happen all at once. But Carl made a new beginning, he took a lot of small steps in the right direction, and he is making a lot of progress. Carl is a new person.

That Was Then and This Is Now

Travel to Minnesota today, and you can meet this couple for coffee. Knowing the backstory and having heard Sharon's descriptions of Carl before, you'd think she was remarried.

That trim, attractive, well-dressed man at her side? That's Carl. The man she sat with in church today during a worship service and praise time? That's him. The guy who's working a steady job and contributing to the household income? Same guy. The gentleman who holds her hand, brings her flowers, takes her out to dinner once in a while, and sometimes rents a romantic movie and brings it home? Her transformed husband.

The same guy who recently was a beer-drinking, stinky, lazy, unemployed bum. He's the same person, but he's also a new man.

Carl's transformation is genuine, and he himself is finding faith in Christ. His makeover is absolutely stunning, and his progress is swift. And all of this began not through any event or incident or situation in his life, but because a transformed wife began walking in the door each night.

As we related this story, we focused on Carl's many obvious faults and failings. Our sympathies were naturally with the poor, unfortunate, godly woman who was stuck with him. Poor lady! She was trapped in a difficult situation, so we might easily overlook some other important details, such as the fact that this wonderful and godly woman had become more than a bit angry. She had allowed bitterness to build up in her heart. She had been repressing a lot of unresolved tension and carrying around a lot of resentment. And as she did these things—ever so gradually—her true inner feelings became visible to others around her, including her husband.

Do you think she walked in the door of her home smiling and whistling a happy tune? Not likely. She was understandably bitter and angry and frustrated. When our hearts are bitter and angry, our faces and tone of voice usually broadcast our condition to those around us. If those people are living with us, they're probably going to figure out that we're not very happy, even if we don't use words.

That was true with Carl and Sharon. For whatever reason, Carl seemed to feel as if living with an angry, frustrated wife gave him the permission he needed to remain a slob, keep on being a jerk, bathe only if he felt like it, and drink beer all day. Sharon's anger somehow enabled him to continue his miserable ways. He was completely unprepared to be married to a positive and optimistic recipient of a spiritual heart transplant.

It blew him away—out of the fridge, into the shower, and down the street to a men's clothing store and a barbershop. It even blew him into a potential employer's office. Experiencing the raw power of a transformed life shattered Carl's self-administered permission to keep on being a jerk. Suddenly, without anyone saying so, he knew in his own heart that the time had come for him to get his act together. And when he got his act together, he went all the way.

All at once? No. All on the same day? As if.

But step-by-step, day after day, he began walking in new directions and becoming a new person. If you had known him before and saw him today, you would not recognize him. But you could pick out Sharon. She's the one smiling with pride and contentment as he opens a door for her. She's the one walking with him to their car after church, discussing where they'll have lunch. Over lunch, they'll be talking about today's sermon. He listened to it, and it really made him think about some things.

This is the true story of a woman who realized that her heart was full of unresolved bitterness. Talking with her counselors, she realized that she'd become an angry, resentful person. She didn't gossip or complain or retaliate outwardly, but her interior life had become stagnant, toxic, and debilitating. Her heart was a mess, and one day she realized it. So she asked God to clean up her heart, and He did.

The real-life outcome was a transformed woman whose new perspective, new attitude, new radiance, and new optimism shattered the complacency of a lazy husband. Carl's paradigm shifted, and he saw himself and his situation in a whole new way.

He woke up and took a shower. He went out and got a job. He started doing his fair share financially. He began paying attention to his appearance. He began paying attention to his wife. All because God changed her heart, and she went right back into the same old situation she'd been trapped in before.

Today, a new husband and a new wife are living in a new marriage. They have the same old house as always, but it sure smells better. And they're making extra payments on the mortgage now, reducing the principal ahead of schedule, because now they're attacking their debts with the blunt force of two full-time incomes instead of just one.

They are making progress in every category. From across the parking lot or across the room you can tell that they love each other. It's not just that she loves him, which is remarkable enough considering all she's been through. He also loves her, and anyone can see it in his expressions and hear it in his words. He is becoming an attentive, romantic husband. He is wooing his wife again, just like the charmer who originally captured her attention.

They are a loving couple—not perfect or finished, but greatly enjoying the journey. And they should enjoy it. After all, they are walking it together.

Carl and Sharon's story raises the question, what else would change if God changed *your* heart?

Becoming Your Husband's Best Friend

Reflections for Your Personal Journey

1. Have you ever found yourself taking sides between a husband and a wife because one of them was so clearly in the wrong? After reading this story, do you realize that sometimes life is a bit more complex than that?

2. Didn't Sharon have every right to be frustrated? Wasn't her anger an entirely normal reaction to her impossibly difficult situation? Shouldn't you be slow to judge her, considering all she is suffering?

3. Were you ahead of the authors in this story? Did you already realize that Sharon's anger and resentment would have been visible to her husband in her attitude and the way she looked at him—or more accurately, the way she avoided him most of the time?

4. Were you surprised by the idea that Sharon's anger gave Carl an excuse to remain ungroomed, unemployed, and unhelpful? Somehow Sharon's disapproval reinforced Carl's tendency to be lazy, out of shape, and out of work even though he never said so and perhaps never even realized it. Did this surprise you?

5. Imagine how Sharon's face changed when her heart changed. How would her mind-set and attitude have changed even though she had to cope with the same circumstances?

6. If you are angry or bitter or resentful, do you think others can tell? Can you effectively hide away your true feelings so that no one knows how you feel?

7. What would happen if you allowed God to purge your heart of the anger and resentment inside you, released your unresolved bitterness, and made yourself available to God's healing touch? (This is not a rhetorical question. Answer it as honestly and completely as you possibly can.)

Resources

This section includes helps and information available from both secular and faith-based sources. We've listed a variety of diverse organizations that support marriages, single adults, divorced persons, blended families, and parents. These organizations share a common desire to be helpful to marriages, families, and those who work with them in order to bring health and stability. However, their inclusion in this brief resource guide does not express or imply our endorsement of their beliefs and practice.

American Association of Christian Counselors

One of the nation's largest networks of counselors, ministers, and resources. Conferences, seminars, continuing education, and training for counselors and others involved in ministry to marriages and families. Online resources and Christian education credits available. National network with local representation widely available.

www.aacc.net

Association of Marriage and Family Ministries

A gathering of ministers and lay leaders who support marriages and families, primarily in local church settings. Provides information and resources about ministries to marriages and families. Open to counselors and professionals as well as all who work with or have interest in marriages. Based in Phoenix, Arizona, metro area, where an annual conference is held.

www.amfmonline.com

Adult Ministries International
Denominational ministry to men, women, and marriages. Based in Lenexa, Kansas, with global presence and resources. Active ongoing training, regional conferences, and online courses.

www.amc.nazarene.org

Center for Marriage and Family Studies
Resources and training to support healthy marriages and strong families. Special attention to military families, clergy families, and blended families. Experts on the post-divorce family landscape and its many challenges. Strong focus on relationship training for couples and families. Key emphasis on support and assistance for counseling before marriage or remarriage. Seminars and conferences on a global basis, plus books and articles to support and strengthen families.

www.MarriageStudies.com

Crown Ministries International
Teaching, training, and resources to help married couples and families make wise financial decisions. Popular radio program available in most markets. Founders include Larry Burkett. Website maintains active links to past broadcasts and podcasts with range of available resources. Focus on managing and reducing debt, budgeting, and accomplishing financial goals.

www.crown.org

Family Life

Speaking, teaching, and training related to strengthening the family. Special events for couples and families include conferences and seminars. See website for calendar of events and resources available in specific locations. Principals include Dennis Rainey.

www.familylife.com

Focus on the Family

Worldwide ministry to families. Based in Colorado Springs. Daily radio broadcast heard in most North American markets and in many global venues. Wide range of resources for most family types including single parents, divorced adults, and remarried couples. Attention to clergy families through a special division. Founders include Dr. James Dobson.

www.focusonthefamily.com

Getting Remarried

Information and resources for those who are considering a remarriage and those who are already remarried or blending a family. Helping remarried couples with decisions related to family life, finances, and more.

www.gettingremarried.com

InStep Ministries

Focus on helping post-divorce adults in various relationships including single parenting, divorce recovery, and blended families. Active interest in aspects of healing, restoration, and hope. Principals are Jeff and Judi Parziale.

www.instepministries.com

Institute for Family Research and Education

Resources and training for couples and families. Attention to all aspects of family life, including parenting, financial challenges, and more. Help for remarried couples and stepfamilies. Ongoing training and support. Directors are Dr. Donald Partridge and Jenetha Partridge.

www.ifre.org

National Association of Social Workers

Maintains a network of social service providers in each state of the United States, organized through its local state chapters. The NASW website maintains a database of information, services, resources, and members that can guide you to locally available providers.

www.naswdc.org

Nazarene Marriage Partnership

Network of professional counselors, authors, ministers, and lay leaders that supports and strengthens marriages and families. Regional conferences and events, online forums and discussions. Has not developed a website but can be accessed via the LinkedIn business network. Focus on creating healthy marriages and strong families. Resources for churches and others who hope to strengthen marriages in their communities.

ParentLife Magazine and Webzine

Monthly magazine for parents and families. Website and blog with updated articles and resources for parents and families. Special attention to single parents and their many challenges. Monthly issues feature a wide range of help for parents, including parents of infants, parents of adolescents, and more. Blog updated frequently. Edited by Jodi Skulley.

Blogs.Lifeway.Com/Blog/Parentlife

Ronald Blue & Company

Resources and information to help couples and families become financially free and achieve their goals. Christian-based financial management services available. Books, articles, and online resources available.

www.RonBlue.com

Smalley Relationship Center

Two generations of Smalleys are now active in helping to support marriages and families. Dr. Gary Smalley is the founder, and his son and daughter-in-law Michael and Amy Smalley are now also actively involved in conferences, seminars, video resources, blogging, and other ways of reaching couples and families with life-changing help and support. Website contains access to calendar of events, online resources, and more.

smalley.cc

www.smalleyonlinestore.com

About the Authors

Authors of 12 books and dozens of articles about marriage, parenting, and issues of family life, Dr. David and Lisa Frisbie serve as executive directors of the Center for Marriage and Family Studies. The Center's primary focus is helping families adapt to crisis and transition, with special attention to post-divorce family dynamics: single parenting, divorce recovery, remarriage issues, and life in a blended family.

The Frisbies speak at retreats and conferences for clergy and spouses and have been instrumental in developing weekend retreats and ongoing curriculum for teenagers of clergy as well as children of missionaries. They also serve military couples and families as seminar speakers and crisis counselors regarding such issues as reentry and post-deployment homecoming and readjustment.

Traveling frequently to speak, teach, and train has taken David and Lisa to all 50 states, 9 provinces and 2 territories of Canada, and more than 30 nations. In addition to Dr. Frisbie's training in marriage and family counseling, he is an ordained minister who has performed almost 400 weddings in diverse locations and across boundaries of culture and language.

Both David and Lisa are frequent contributors to *ParentLife* magazine and have been named and quoted in *USA Today*, the *New York Times*, and other print outlets. They have appeared on numerous local television and radio stations and have been interviewed by Chuck Bentley of *MoneyLife* (Crown Ministries) and Jim Burns on his popular radio broadcast *HomeWord*. They can be heard on drive-time interviews in Seattle, Detroit, Tulsa, Yuma, and other markets.

Several previous books by Dr. and Mrs. Frisbie have been selected as recommended resources by Willow Creek Community Church, Focus on the Family, Concerned Women for America, Billy Graham's Bookstore at the Cove, and numerous other organizations and ministries. Their writing has won many awards and endorsements. They serve on the faculty of an annual writing conference in Southern California and frequently present seminars and workshops at other conferences for ministers, counselors, and writers.

Dr. David Frisbie serves as an adjunct faculty member at Southern Nazarene University, where he teaches family studies and gerontology in the graduate and professional degree programs.

Married for 30 years, David and Lisa teach, speak, and write as a team. By long established practice and strong personal preference, they travel and serve together.

- To inquire about book signings and author appearances, contact Laurie Tomlinson at Laurie@keymgc.com.
- To inquire about booking the authors for speaking engagements, contact Lisa Douglas at mountainmediagroup@yahoo.com.
- The authors maintain a writing blog at www.emergingintofaith.com.
- Visit the Center for Marriage and Family Studies website at www.MarriageStudies.com.
- Contact the Frisbies directly at Director@MarriageStudies.com.
- More information about these authors is available at www.LinkedIn.com/in/davidandlisafrisbie.

Partial Bibliography
Couples Night Out: Making Cents DVD and CD (Group Publishing)
Happily Remarried: Blending a Family (Harvest House)

Making a Marriage (Beacon Hill Press)

Marriage Ministry in the 21st Century (Group Publishing)

Moving Forward After Divorce (Harvest House)

Raising Great Kids on Your Own (Harvest House)

Salga Adelante Despues del Divorcio (Strang Communications)

The Soul-Mate Marriage (Harvest House)

Work & Witness Journeybook (Beacon Hill Press)

Construyendo un Matrimonia (Casa Nazarena)

To learn more about other Harvest House books
or to read sample chapters, log on to our website:

www.harvesthousepublishers.com